ANNE FIROR SCOTT

editor of this volume in the
Eyewitness Accounts of American History Series
is Associate Professor of History,
Duke University.

Author of *The Southern Lady* and several other books
on the status of women,
she is former chairman of the North Carolina
Governor's Commission on the Status of Women.
She was appointed by President Johnson to
the Citizens Advisory Council on the Status of Women.

D0029084

THE AMERICAN WOMAN

Who Was She?

Edited by

Anne Firor Scott

Prentice-Hall, Inc. A SPECTRUM BOOK *Englewood Cliffs, N. J.*

For Becky

Contents

4. REFORM   88

5. WOMEN AND MEN:
MARRIAGE, FAMILY, SEX   129

THE AMERICAN WOMAN
Who Was She?

Introduction

Poets and novelists rarely overlook women. Historians often do. Frequently they write as if half the human race did not exist, and this despite the enormous amounts of time, thought, emotion, and print that are periodically devoted to debating what women should or should not do, what they can or cannot be, and despite the fact that many of these debates are carried on by men. There are fat textbooks in American history which mention women three or four times, and a good deal more attention is often paid to a single political leader or some short-lived political movement than to the accomplishments of women in three hundred years. It is particularly intriguing that social and economic historians of the past century have overlooked women, for during that time one of the most impressive social and economic facts has been the rapid change in the part women have played in the society and the economy.

One day perhaps an inquiring psychologist will explain the extreme reluctance of American historians to recognize that women have been here too, and when that time comes the answer will be, in part, that the historians were men. Male historians share society's attitudes toward women, and add a few of their own. They carry a heavy baggage of assumptions, usually unacknowledged and unexamined, about the importance of women in history. It is time they began to examine these assumptions, to correct the biases built into their work, and to revise their accounts of historical events accordingly.

The theme of this book is the relationship between the changing role of women in American society and the changes in women's education, in their patterns of work, their participation in reform movements, and their views of family life. The following series of documents covers developments in these areas from the middle of the nineteenth century to the present. In some of them men speak about women, but more often women speak for themselves in letters, memoirs, essays, and speeches. Viewing these selections together, a surprising number of ideas which have been much discussed recently turn out to have been foreshadowed a century ago as American women began making a concerted effort to secure better education, professional opportunities, and the right to vote.

Included here are excerpts from the writings of the leading theoreticians of feminism: Antoinette Brown Blackwell, Charlotte Perkins Gilman, Anna Garlin Spencer and Carrie Chapman Catt, for example. There are also selections written by little-known individuals who thought about women's needs and helped pioneer new patterns. Other selections are included because they sum up particular developments, such as the opening of opportunities in education or the changing pattern of women's work. Taken together they form a mosaic showing how women fitted into society, how society looked at them, the restraints upon women's activities and development, the way these restraints were embodied in social norms and laws, and the changes which education and professional opportunities, as well as industrialization and urbanization, helped to bring about.

Although the past century has witnessed enormous change in the lives of American women, the end is not yet in sight. Some selections here suggest the direction of future change. In the past, for example, women who felt a need for personal and professional development beyond the traditional home-and-mother role either decided to forego the latter in favor of the former, or made heroic efforts to combine the two. Today some women are saying that the traditional family structure is incompatible with true freedom for women, and instead of accepting the structure as given and adjusting their own lives accordingly, they speak of changing the structure. The way this issue is resolved will be greatly influenced by external events of which we are as yet only dimly aware. The pressure to curtail population growth may do more to broaden opportunities for women than all the oratory and agitation and organization of the past hundred years.

Long ago, Abigail Adams enjoined her husband, then engaged

in writing a constitution for a new nation, to "remember the ladies. . . ." It seems strange that women should need to remind men in this way, but the injunction has been needed ever since. Even when men have thought *about* women they have been inclined to believe that they must think *for* them as well. On one occasion in the nineteenth century men called a meeting to discuss the rights of women—and would not permit any woman to speak. Today's radical feminists often bar men from their meetings, a symbolic rejection of the old pattern.

It is all very well to be loved, admired, flattered, and praised for being beautiful and feminine. This book shows, however, that women want something more. They want to be respected for their talents and abilities, when they have them, and not to be patronized as beings whose only possible excellence lies in bearing children and being properly pleasing to men. The women who speak here are concerned with rights, with the broadening of opportunities, with the development of new options in life styles, and with a desire to stand alongside men and receive the respect of society when they have earned it. As the numbers of such women increase it may become less necessary to enjoin men to "remember the ladies. . . ." They won't be able to forget them.

Because women's history has been so little attended to the task of the editor is both easier and more difficult than in other fields. It is easier because the materials are not shop-worn: few of the selections in this book have been reprinted anywhere. It is harder because one must make choices, and in making one selection, pass up many others. To those who find their appetites whetted I recommend some of the classics of the feminist movement: Elizabeth Cady Stanton's incomparable *Eighty Years and More*; the six-volume *History of Woman Suffrage* compiled by Mrs. Stanton, Susan B. Anthony, Matilda Joslyn Gage, and Ida Husted Harper, which is a virtually inexhaustible treasure house of women's history; Charlotte Perkins Gilman's *Women and Economics*; Anna Garlin Spencer's *Woman's Share in Social Culture*; and Mary Grey Peck's biography of Carrie Chapman Catt. The best new book available is Aileen Kraditor's *Up From the Pedestal*, a superb collection of documents. For background the best thing yet available is Eleanor Flexner's *Century of Struggle*.

Chapter 1

The Background

Although this book centers on women in the century after the Civil War when the United States was experiencing ever more rapid technological and social changes, it is necessary to know a little of what had gone before. In colonial times American women had a hard life, but considerable opportunity. Women's work was important (as the Virginia assembly recognized almost as soon as the first settlement began, when it agreed to give grants of land to women as well as men). As the colonial society took shape in the seventeenth and early eighteenth centuries, women could be found doing all kinds of things: speaking for themselves in courts of law, running print shops and newspapers, inns and schools, practicing medicine, and supervising plantations. In addition, of course, nearly all women made clothes; grew, preserved, and prepared food; cared for livestock; and taught children.[1]

After the Revolution this pattern continued on farms and in rural communities, but in the growing towns wives of prosperous merchants could afford to imitate English standards and live as they thought ladies lived. In the more organized society of the early nineteenth century, law, medicine, and teaching became professions carried on solely by men. Some women of wealth and leisure had time to turn their attention to reform movements, including the woman's rights movement to improve their own legal status. At about the same time another kind of life style for another kind of woman came into being in the textile mills of New England,

1. See Julia Cherry Spruill, *Women's Life and Work in the Southern Colonies* (Chapel Hill, 1938) and Elizabeth Dexter, *Colonial Women of Affairs* (New York, 1924).

4

where country girls were operating the machines for wages lower than those paid men for similar kinds of work.

Nineteenth-century Americans exhibited a good deal of anxiety about the question of "woman's sphere." What were the things appropriate for women to do? The most conservative view was that God had created women to take care of men and children, and that whenever they took part in public activities they were being unladylike. Women were seen as gentle, pious, sentimental, emotional—and not very bright. The law reflected this view of woman as an inferior being, so that a married woman had no legal standing—she could not make a will, sell property (even though she might have been an heiress), or ask for a divorce. No women could vote or sit on juries. Education was primarily for boys, higher education entirely so.

Some women found these attitudes and restrictions galling. Sarah Grimké, for example, left her South Carolina home and went north to fight slavery. When she spoke in public about her experiences as a South Carolina slaveholder she was criticized, when she was not jeered, for breaking out of woman's sphere. She responded with a carefully reasoned book, *Letters on the Equality of the Sexes,* which argued that women could never do their fair share of the world's work until they were educated to do more than amuse and take care of men. Other women in the abolitionist movement were appalled by the similarity between their own legal position and that of slaves. An extraordinary group, led by Elizabeth Cady Stanton and Lucretia Mott, called a Woman's Rights Convention in Seneca Falls, New York in 1848 and laid down the opening salvo in a battle that has not ended yet. The declaration printed below is the key both to specific grievances and to women's feelings about their deprivation.

WOMAN'S RIGHTS CONVENTION—A convention to discuss the social, civil, and religious condition and rights of woman, will be held in the Wesleyan Chapel, at Seneca Falls, N. Y., on Wednesday and Thursday, the nineteenth and twentieth of July, current; commencing at 10 o'clock A.M. During the first day the meeting will be exclusively for women, who are earnestly invited to attend. The public generally

E. C. *Stanton,* S. B. *Anthony, and* M. J. *Gage,* History of Woman Suffrage *(Rochester: Susan B. Anthony, 1881), vol. 1, pp. 67–71.*

are invited to be present on the second day, when Lucretia Mott, of Philadelphia, and other ladies and gentlemen, will address the convention.

This call, without signature, was issued by Lucretia Mott, Martha C. Wright, Elizabeth Cady Stanton, and Mary Ann McClintock. At this time Mrs. Mott was visiting her sister Mrs. Wright, at Auburn, and attending the Yearly Meeting of Friends in Western New York. Mrs. Stanton, having recently removed from Boston to Seneca Falls, finding the most congenial associations in Quaker families, met Mrs. Mott incidentally for the first time since her residence there. They at once returned to the topic they had so often discussed, walking arm in arm in the streets of London, and Boston, "the propriety of holding a woman's convention." These four ladies, sitting round the tea-table of Richard Hunt, a prominent Friend near Waterloo, decided to put their long-talked-of resolution into action, and before the twilight deepened into night, the call was written, and sent to the *Seneca County Courier*. On Sunday morning they met in Mrs. McClintock's parlor to write their declaration, resolutions, and to consider subjects for speeches. As the convention was to assemble in three days, the time was short for such productions; but having no experience in the *modus operandi* of getting up conventions, nor in that kind of literature, they were quite innocent of the herculean labors they proposed. On the first attempt to frame a resolution, to crowd a complete thought, clearly and concisely, into three lines, they felt as helpless and hopeless as if they had been suddenly asked to construct a steam engine. And the humiliating fact may as well now be recorded that before taking the initiative step, those ladies resigned themselves to a faithful perusal of various masculine productions. The reports of Peace, Temperance, and Anti-Slavery conventions were examined, but all alike seemed too tame and pacific for the inauguration of a rebellion such as the world had never before seen. They knew women had wrongs, but how to state them was the difficulty, and this was increased from the fact that they themselves were fortunately organized and conditioned; they were neither "sour old maids," "childless women," nor "divorced wives," as the newspapers declared them to be. While they had felt the insults incident to sex, in many ways, as every proud, thinking woman must, in the laws, religion, and literature of the world, and in the invidious and degrading sentiments and customs of all nations, yet they had not in their own experience endured the coarser forms of tyranny resulting from unjust laws, or association with immoral and unscrupulous men, but they had souls large enough to feel the wrongs of others, without being scarified in their own flesh.

After much delay, one of the circle took up the Declaration of 1776, and read it aloud with much spirit and emphasis, and it was at once decided to adopt the historic document, with some slight changes such as substituting "all men" for "King George." Knowing that women must have more to complain of than men under any circumstances possibly could, and seeing the Fathers had eighteen grievances, a protracted search was made through statute books, church usages, and the customs of society to find that exact number. Several well-disposed men assisted in collecting the grievances, until, with the announcement of the eighteenth, the women felt they had enough to go before the world with a good case. One youthful lord remarked, "Your grievances must be grievous indeed, when you are obliged to go to books in order to find them out."

The eventful day dawned at last, and crowds in carriages and on foot wended their way to the Wesleyan church. When those having charge of the declaration, the resolutions, and several volumes of the statutes of New York arrived on the scene, lo! the door was locked. However, an embryo professor of Yale College was lifted through an open window to unbar the door; that done, the church was quickly filled. It had been decided to have no men present, but as they were already on the spot, and as the women who must take the responsibility of organizing the meeting, and leading the discussions, shrank from doing either, it was decided, in a hasty council round the alter, that this was an occasion when men might make themselves preeminently useful. It was agreed they should remain, and take the laboring oar through the convention.

James Mott, tall and dignified, in Quaker costume, was called to the chair; Mary McClintock appointed secretary, Frederick Douglass, Samuel Tillman, Ansel Bascom, E. W. Capron, and Thomas McClintock took part throughout in the discussions. Lucretia Mott, accustomed to public speaking in the Society of Friends, stated the objects of the convention, and in taking a survey of the degraded condition of woman the world over, showed the importance of inaugurating some movement for her education and elevation.

Elizabeth and Mary McClintock, and Mrs. Stanton, each read a well-written speech; Martha Wright read some satirical articles she had published in the daily papers answering the diatribes on woman's sphere. Ansel Bascom, who had been a member of the constitutional convention recently held in Albany, spoke at length on the property bill for married women, just passed the legislature, and the discussion on woman's rights in that convention. Samuel Tillman, a young student of law, read a series of the most exasperating statutes for women, from English and American jurists, all reflecting the *tender mercies* of men toward their wives, in taking care of their property and protecting them in their civil rights.

The declaration having been freely discussed by many present, was reread by Mrs. Stanton, and with some slight amendments adopted.

Declaration of sentiments

When, in the course of human events, it becomes necessary for one portion of the family of man to assume among the people of the earth a position different from that which they have hitherto occupied, but one to which the laws of nature and of nature's God entitle them, a decent respect to the opinions of mankind requires that they should declare the causes that impel them to such a course.

We hold these truths to be self-evident: that all men and women are created equal; that they are endowed by their Creator with certain inalienable rights; that among these are life, liberty, and the pursuit of happiness; that to secure these rights governments are instituted, deriving their just powers from the consent of the governed. Whenever any form of government becomes destructive of these ends, it is the right of those who suffer from it to refuse allegiance to it, and to insist upon the institution of a new government, laying its foundation on such principles, and organizing its powers in such form, as to them shall seem most likely to effect their safety and happiness. Prudence, indeed, will dictate that governments long established should not be changed for light and transient causes; and accordingly all experience hath shown that mankind are more disposed to suffer, while evils are sufferable, than to right themselves by abolishing the forms to which they were accustomed. But when a long train of abuses and usurpations, pursuing invariably the same object evinces a design to reduce them under absolute despotism, it is their duty to throw off such government, and to provide new guards for their future security. Such has been the patient sufferance of the women under this government, and such is now the necessity which constrains them to demand the equal station to which they are entitled.

The history of mankind is a history of repeated injuries and usurpations on the part of man toward woman, having in direct object the establishment of an absolute tyranny over her. To prove this, let facts be submitted to a candid world.

He has never permitted her to exercise her inalienable right to the elective franchise.

He has compelled her to submit to laws, in the formation of which she had no voice.

He has withheld from her rights which are given to the most ignorant and degraded men—both natives and foreigners.

Having deprived her of this first right of a citizen, the elective franchise, thereby leaving her without representation in the halls of legislation, he has oppressed her on all sides.

He has made her, if married, in the eye of the law, civilly dead.

He has taken from her all right in property, even to the wages she earns.

He has made her, morally, an irresponsible being, as she can commit many crimes with impunity, provided they be done in the presence of her husband. In the covenant of marriage, she is compelled to promise obedience to her husband, he becoming, to all intents and purposes, her master—the law giving him power to deprive her of her liberty, and to administer chastisement.

He has so framed the laws of divorce, as to what shall be the proper causes, and in case of separation, to whom the guardianship of the children shall be given, as to be wholly regardless of the happiness of women—the law, in all cases, going upon a false supposition of the supremacy of man, and giving all power into his hands.

After depriving her of all rights as a married woman, if single, and the owner of property, he has taxed her to support a government which recognizes her only when her property can be made profitable to it.

He has monopolized nearly all the profitable employments, and from those she is permitted to follow, she receives but a scanty remuneration. He closes against her all the avenues to wealth and distinction which he considers most honorable to himself. As a teacher of theology, medicine, or law, she is not known.

He has denied her the facilities for obtaining a thorough education, all colleges being closed against her.

He allows her in Church, as well as State, but a subordinate position, claiming Apostolic authority for her exclusion from the ministry, and, with some exceptions, from any public participation in the affairs of the Church.

He has created a false public sentiment by giving to the world a different code of morals for men and women, by which moral delinquencies which exclude women from society, are not only tolerated, but deemed of little account in man.

He has usurped the prerogative of Jehovah himself, claiming it as his right to assign for her a sphere of action, when that belongs to her conscience and to her God.

He has endeavored, in every way that he could, to destroy her confidence in her own powers, to lessen her self-respect, and to make her willing to lead a dependent and abject life.

Now, in view of this entire disfranchisement of one-half the people of this country, their social and religious degradation—in view of the unjust laws above mentioned, and because women do feel themselves aggrieved, oppressed, and fraudulently deprived of their most sacred rights, we insist that they have immediate admission to all the rights and privileges which belong to them as citizens of the United States.

In entering upon the great work before us, we anticipate no small amount of misconception, misrepresentation, and ridicule; but we shall use every instrumentality within our power to effect our object. We shall employ agents, circulate tracts, petition the State and National legislatures, and endeavor to enlist the pulpit and the press in our behalf. We hope this Convention will be followed by a series of Conventions embracing every part of the country.

Chapter 2

Woman's Work

Most societies divide work between men and women, though the reasons for the particular way "woman's work" is separated from that of men are not always apparent. In some places women do all the hard labor while men sit under the trees and drink the beer that women make. In others, women are in charge of the family finances and men concentrate on religion and learning. In this country, men wash dishes in restaurants, but often think it is inappropriate to do so at home. Women are permitted to teach but seldom to preach. It is hard to explain many of these divisions except on the basis of custom.

During most of human history most people have had little choice of what work they would do. Only in recent times, as the margin of wealth has increased, have we begun to think that people should do the kind of work which best fits their talents, personalities and psychological needs. And even now, in our society, many people think that *all* women are naturally suited to be housewives, and that when they do other kinds of things, whether from necessity or choice, they are in danger of becoming "unwomanly." This widespread conviction has helped to mask the fact that in each successive decade of industrialization, more and more women do work away from home. Today half of all women between the ages of 18 and 64 are earning wages, and 38 percent of all workers are women.

The debate over women's work has run along two different lines. The first pertains to their wages and working conditions, which have always been inferior to those of men in equivalent positions. The second has had to do with the more fortunate women who wanted to widen their options, who objected to being forced into marriage simply because they could be supported and who persistently asked for the right to enter the professions. This second thread is closely related to the demand for better education, which is treated in the next section. Although the issue of equal pay for equal work was at a different level of dollars and cents for the professional woman, it was still present. In 1965–66 the National Education Association found a 16 percent difference in median salaries of men and women in higher education. In 1968 the Census Bureau reported that the median income of men with five years or more of college was $12,803 while women of the same educational level had a median income of $8,257.

THE SENATE INVESTIGATES "WOMEN'S WORK"

In 1910 the United States Senate published nineteen volumes on Women and Child Wage Earners in the United States—itself an indication of how important wage-earning women had become. Volume IX was devoted entirely to women, and its introduction summarized the experience of the nineteenth century.

The history of women in industry in the United States is the story of a great industrial readjustment, which has not only carried woman's work from the home to the factory, but has changed its economic character from unpaid production for home consumption to gainful employment in the manufacture of articles for sale. Women have always worked, and their work has probably always been quite as important a factor in the total economy of society as it is today. But during the nineteenth century a transformation occurred in their economic position and in the character and conditions of their work. Their unpaid services have been transformed into paid services, their work has been removed from the home to the factory and workshop, their range of possible employment has been increased and at the same time their monopoly of their traditional occupations has been destroyed. The individuality of their work has been lost in a standardized product.

U.S., Congress, Senate, Report on the Condition of Women and Children Wage Earners in the United States, Senate Document no. 645, 61st Cong., 2d Sess., 1910, IX: 11–13. Volume IX, History of Women in Industry in the United States, was prepared by Helen L. Sumner, Ph.D.

The story of woman's work in gainful employments is a story of constant changes or shiftings of work and workshop, accompanied by long hours, low wages, insanitary conditions, overwork, and the want on the part of the woman of training, skill, and vital interest in her work. It is a story of monotonous machine labor, of division and subdivision of tasks until the woman, like the traditional tailor who is called the ninth part of a man, is merely a fraction, and that rarely as much even as a tenth part, of an artisan. It is a story, moreover, of underbidding, of strikebreaking, of the lowering of standards for men breadwinners.

In certain industries and certain localities women's unions have raised the standard of wages. The opening of industrial schools and business colleges, too, though affecting almost exclusively the occupations entered by the daughters of middle-class families who have only recently begun to pass from home work to the industrial field, has at least enabled these few girls to keep from further swelling the vast numbers of the unskilled. The evil of long hours and in certain cases other conditions which lead to overstrain, such as the constant standing of saleswomen, have been made the subject of legislation. The decrease of strain due to shorter hours has, however, been in part nullified by increased speed of machinery and other devices designed to obtain the greatest possible amount of labor from each woman. Nevertheless, the history of woman's work in this country shows that legislation has been the only force which has improved the working conditions of any large number of women wage earners. Aside from the little improvement that has been effected in the lot of working women, the most surprising fact brought out in this study is the long period of time through which large numbers of women have worked under conditions which have involved not only great hardships to themselves but shocking waste to the community.

Changes in Occupations of Women

The transfer of women from non-wage-earning home work to gainful occupations is evident to the most superficial observer, and it is well known that most of this transfer has been effected since the beginning of the nineteenth century. In 1870 it was found that 14.7 percent of the female population sixteen years of age and over were breadwinners, and by 1900 the percentage was 20.6

percent. During the period for which statistics exist, moreover, the movement toward the increased employment of women in gainful pursuits was clear and distinct in all sections of the country and was even more marked among the native-born than among the foreign-born. It must be borne in mind, however, that even in colonial days there were many women who worked for wages, especially at spinning, weaving, the sewing trades, and domestic service. Many women, too, carried on business on their own account in the textile and sewing trades and also in such industries as the making of blackberry brandy. The wage labor of women is as old as the country itself and has merely increased in importance. The amount, however, of unremunerated home work performed by women must still be considerably larger than the amount of gainful labor, for even in 1900 only about one-fifth of the women sixteen years of age and over were breadwinners.

Along with the decrease in the importance of unremunerated home labor and the increase in the importance of wage labor has gone a considerable amount of shifting of occupations. Under the old domestic system the work of the woman was to spin, to do a large part of the weaving, to sew, to knit; in general, to make most of the clothing worn by the family, to embroider tapestry in the days and regions where there was time for art, to cook, to brew ale and wine, to clean, and to perform the other duties of the domestic servant. These things women have always done. But machines have now come in to aid in all these industries—machines which in some cases have brought in their train men operatives and in other cases have enormously increased the productive power of the individual and have made it necessary for many women, who under the old régime, like Priscilla, would have calmly sat by the window spinning, to hunt other work. One kind of spinning is now done by men only. Men tailors make every year thousands of women's suits. Men dressmakers and even milliners are common. Men make our bread and brew our ale and do much of the work of the steam laundry where our clothes are washed. Recently, too, men have learned to clean our houses by the vacuum process.

Before the introduction of spinning machinery and the sewing machine the supply of female labor appears never to have been excessive. But the spinning jenny threw out of employment thousands of "spinsters," who were obliged to restort to sewing as the only other occupation to which they were in any way trained. This accounts for the terrible pressure in the clothing trades during the early decades of the nineteenth century. Later on, before any readjustment of women's work had been effected, the sewing machine was introduced, which enormously increased the pressure of competition among women workers. Shortly after the substitution of machinery for the spinning wheel the women of certain localities in Massachusetts found an outlet in binding shoes—an opportunity opened to them by the division of labor and by the development of the ready-made trade. But when the sewing machine was introduced this field, at least for a time, was again contracted. Under this pressure, combined with the rapid development of wholesale industry and division of labor, women have been pressed into other industries, almost invariably in the first instance into the least skilled and most poorly paid occupations. This has gone on until there is now scarcely an industry which does not employ women. Thus woman's sphere has expanded, and its former boundaries can now be determined only by observing the degree of popular condemnation which follows their employment in particular industries.

AN OVERVIEW, 1800–1900

In the following selection an economics professor at Barnard College who has been interested in labor problems and in the effects of technology on our society gives a more detailed picture of women's work in the nineteenth century. The reaction of male-dominated trade unions to the entrance of women into industry is a facet of women's struggle for equality that is often overlooked.

The accompanying table reveals some of the end results of a century of change in women's work:

The table reveals first of all that, although in 1900 women were "a new economic factor"—marginal members of the nation's labor force, more than five million, or about 1 in every 5 in the female population ten years of age and over, had become paid employees, and that nearly 18 in every 100 wage earners were

Elizabeth Faulkner Baker, Technology and Woman's Work (*New York: Columbia University Press, 1964*), *pp. 75–79. Reprinted by permission of the publisher.*

GAINFULLY EMPLOYED WOMEN IN 1900

	10 years of age and over	16 years of age and over	Percent of all employed women		Women as a percent of all employees 16 years and over
			10 years and over	15 years and over	
Total	5,319,397	4,833,630	100.00	100.00	17.7
Agriculture	977,336	770,055	18.4	16.2	8.3
Professional service	430,597	429,497	8.1	8.6	34.2
(teachers and professors in colleges, etc.)		(327,206)		(6.5)	(73.4)
Domestic and personal service	2,095,449	1,953,467	39.4	40.2	36.8
Trade and transportation	503,347	481,159	9.4	9.9	10.4
Manufacturing and mechanical pursuits	1,312,668	1,199,452	24.7	25.1	17.6

Female population 10 years and over: 28,246,384—18.8 percent employed
Female population 16 years and over: 23,485,559—20.6 percent employed
Male population 16 years and over: 24,851,013—90.5 percent employed

Sources: Sumner, *Women in Industry*, pp. 18, 246, 247, 254, 259; U.S. Bureau of the Census, *Statistics of Women at Work*, pp. 9, 10, 32, 109; Abbott and Breckinridge [*Women in Industry* (New York: D. Appleton, 1928)], p. 25.

women sixteen years and over. This means that the number of employed women had tripled in thirty years.

Much the largest proportion of these women and girls were still in domestic and personal service—more than 2,000,000 or about 40 in every 100. But it should be noted that the proportion had dropped from 58 in 100 in 1870, and that in the last decade of the century more males than females entered this form of employment. It is also well to recall that even in 1900 nearly 12,000 graduate nurses were reported as domestic and personal servants, and that hotels and restaurants had drawn many women and girls away from household work.

The second largest number of working women and girls after a century of change were in manufacturing and mechanical pursuits—more than 1,300,000, approaching one-fourth of all, which was four times as many as in 1870. This is where women's paid work began, it will be recalled. They had been dispossessed of their work at home by textile machines that stimulated investment

for private profit in an ambitious new country rich in natural resources. Thus "doomed to idleness," they worked in cotton mills
to earn a living or to help support a family, and to free men for
work in the fields. In varying degrees women were also desirable
workers in the manufacture of woolen and worsted goods, silk
goods, and hosiery and knitwear.

The early invention of the principle of interchangeable parts
that brought mass production by semiskilled and unskilled workers
at specialized machines marked a second great step in women's
work. Even if they had been accepted as apprentices to the skilled
trades, most girls were reluctant to spend four years in training
because they expected to be married and have children. In other
words they were said not to take their work *con amore,* but they
could learn to tend machines in a short time, and they were quick
and dexterous.

An early and highly important product of the application of
the principle of interchangeable parts was the sewing machine,
which did for women in the clothing trades what machines had
done in the textile industry—transferred their work from home
to factory. In fact, we have noted that in every census year considerably more than half of all employed women and girls were
in the cloth and clothing trades, including the binding of boots
and shoes, which was new to them. Their work had changed in
character, but not in amount or even in intensity.

As automatic machinery and quantity production made division
of labor possible in other industries, and as immigration increased
at a time when textile machines were becoming heavier and more
complicated, women were drawn into numerous other occupations
which they had not known before. For example, the manufacture
of clocks and watches and other metal products was considered
"admirably adapted to the female sex" because of nimble fingers
and sensitive touch. And we may recall that in 1890 the United
States Commissioner of Labor reported that women were employed
in all but 9 out of the 369 groups of manufacturing and mechanical
industries.

For the most part, men in labor unions resisted the entrance of
women into their trades because they associated women's occupations with the coming of machines, which threatened their
security as craftsmen. Moreover, women accepted jobs as strike-
breakers at times, and took what wages they could get. An out-

standing example of such a conflict was in the manufacture of cigars and cigarettes, the result of which was that by the close of the century 53,000 women and girls were at work in the tobacco industry—38 in each 100 wage earners. Women fared far less well in the organized printing trades, however, except for the semi-skilled operations in bookbinding, where they comprised about half of all in that trade.

The third largest group of employed women and girls at the turn of the century were on the farm—977,000 ten years of age and over, or 18 percent of all employed females, more than 770,000 of them at least sixteen years of age. The number of women and girls had increased twice as fast as the number of men and boys. However, less than 9 in every 100 farm workers were women in 1900.

Coming to the Twelfth Census report on women in the professions we find that, while only one in three persons in the entire division was a woman, more than 73 in each 100 teachers were women. Consider this outcome in the light of the earlier assertion that an educated wife was "an infringement upon the domain of man."

Finally, we look at the Trade and Transportation Census for 1900 where 10 percent of all employees sixteen years of age and over were women. But our table cannot reveal that in the last thirty years of the century the number of women and girls in this division soared from 19,000 to more than 503,000—some 2,700 percent. More than nine out of ten of these "white-collar" workers were saleswomen, telegraph and telephone operators, stenographers and typists, clerks and copyists, bookkeepers and accountants. The 140,000 saleswomen may otherwise have been domestic servants, seamstresses, or "working women" in some other congested occupation. But the commercial and clerical jobs—especially those created by the invention of the telephone, the typewriter, and other office devices—drew "middle-class" women and girls away from domesticity into paid work. These young women had had more schooling than other employed females except for those in the professional services. More girls than boys were high school graduates, and many of them also received special training so that business executives found themselves both surprised and pleased to have them around.

Looking back over the century, then, we witnessed in the early decades women and girls of all classes—"educated" and uneducated

—entering the factory because machines had taken much of their work away. Again in the final decades we found all classes at paid work, but with the difference that four-fifths of them were employed outside the factory. As railroads and business combinations expanded production and trade throughout the nation, new office and commercial devices had seemed to answer the prayers of those who had been asking what to do with daughters. In addition, nursing had become "woman's work," and more women than men were teachers. "The advance of women, during the last hundred years or so, is a phenomenon unparalleled in history," wrote a prominent feminist and reformer.

> Never before has so large a class made as much progress in so small a time. From the harem to the forum is a long step, but she has taken it. From the ignorant housewife to the president of a college is a long step, but she has taken it. From the penniless dependent to the wholly self-supporting and often other-supporting businesswoman, is a long step, but she has taken it. She who knew so little is now the teacher; she who could do so little is now the efficient and varied producer; she who cared only for her own flesh and blood is now active in all wide good works around the world. She who was confined to the house now travels freely, the foolish has become wise, and the timid brave.[1]

Nevertheless, woman's place in American society was one of the great unsolved questions of the day. . . .

THE HOME LIVES OF FACTORY WOMEN

What realities lay behind the statistics? An articulate feminist reported some of her observations of the lives of factory women. Rheta Childe Dorr was a Nebraska woman who had found domestic life stifling and left her husband to become a newspaper reporter and a war correspondent. In 1924 she published her autobiography, from which this selection is reprinted:

Fall River gave me another view of what the Industrial Revolution had done to women. In the cotton mills whole families

---

Rheta Childe Dorr, A Woman of Fifty (*New York: Funk & Wagnalls, 1924*), *pp. 188–89. Reprinted by permission of the publisher.*

1. Charlotte Perkins Gilman, *The Home: Its Work and Influence* (New York: McClure, Phillips & Co., 1903), p. 324.

worked together, mostly the same tasks and always the same hours. All worked, but when the whistles blew and the toilers poured out of the mills and hurried to their homes, what happened? The women of the mills went on working. They cooked and served meals, washed dishes, cleaned the house, tucked the children into bed, and after that sewed, mended or did a family washing. Eleven o'clock at night seemed the conventional hour for clothesline pulleys to begin creaking all over town. The men of the family were asleep by this time after an evening spent in smoking, drinking, talking union politics with cronies in barrooms or corner groceries, or placidly nodding at home over a newspaper, their stockinged feet resting on a chair or a porch rail. Working men always seem to rest in their stockinged feet, and very sensibly too, when you think of it. I have heard women describing a period of unemployment say: "He ain't had his shoes on for two weeks."

I never heard of a working woman or the wife of a working man who kept her shoes off for two weeks. In Fall River a woman in the mills and at home worked an average of fourteen hours a day and had babies between times. The babies could not be taken to the mills, and as soon as the mothers were able to leave their beds they relegated the care of the babies to some grandmother, herself a broken down mill-worker, or to the baby-farms in which the town abounded. Of course the babies fared ill under this system, the mortality rate among them being very high. In summer, a reputable physician told me, it sometimes reached the appalling rate of 50 percent of all births. I am writing of conditions of some years back and these may be better now. But they cannot be much better, for women still work all day in the mills and half the night at home, and healthy babies cannot be born of such overworked mothers.

The whole panorama of women's lives in that mill-town gave me the impression that the human race was on its way to the abyss.

LOOKING FOR WORK

Among the working women who show up as statistics in the previous selections there were always a large contingent of immigrants who had come to this country hoping to find better work and more pay than they could get at home. Elizabeth Hasanovitz left Russia because she could see no possible chance for remunerative work there, came first to Canada, and then moved on to New York. She described her first experience with job-hunting.

So the last week of September, 1912, I arrived in New York, with eight dollars in my pocket and just one address, given me by the Socialist-Territorialist Party to their New York headquarters.

In truth, I was full of fear all the way, a girl all alone in New York, not knowing the language.

"Nonsense, I am old enough to take care of myself." I tried to quiet my fears as I had tried to quiet my mother's.

When I stepped out of the train at the Grand Central Station, not then completed, a few middle-aged ladies, travellers' guides from the YWCA, stopped me, asking me if I wished assistance. But not knowing who they were, I looked at them with distrust.

I went out on the street with my heavy suitcase, making my way among the various porters, who offered their assistance, and, seeing my look of suspicion, showed me their badges to reassure me. But I went to a policeman, who put me on a streetcar, and I found the office on Delancy Street, where members of the staff received me kindly.

Luckily, I found a job in Brooklyn, in a knitting factory, to sew pockets on sweaters—the same work I had done in Canada. It was the height of the season. Ten dollars a week was considered good pay.

I found a room on Eighth Street; also a roommate. I managed to live on five dollars a week—one dollar for my share of the room rent, three dollars for food, and one dollar for general expenses. The other five I began to save. I wanted to save enough to buy a ticket for my brother so that he might come, and together we might bring the rest of the family. . . .

Five weeks passed, five happy weeks. I had already twenty-five dollars saved. My constant thought was, "I shall soon be able to buy a ticket and send for my brother."

But fate decided differently. On Monday of my sixth week, when I came into the shop the forelady came over to me and announced: "It has got slow, Sugar Face! there will be no work for you.—But what do you care for work?" she added laughingly.

Elizabeth Hasanovitz, One of Them (*Boston and New York: Houghton Mifflin Co., 1918*), *pp. 15–16, 18–21. Reprinted by permission of the publisher.*

She left me with no further explanation. I went over to the foreman to ask for a reason. He explained to me that it had turned slow and the boss kept only the quickest and cheapest hands, and the forelady was the one to select the fittest.

So I unexpectedly lost my job. What was I to do now?

With my lunch of two buttered rolls in my hands, I returned home.

New York with its slack season, New York and starvation stared me in the face. But I refused to be discouraged. I had come to New York with eight dollars in my pocket. Now I had twenty-five. Am I not better off now? Did I not prepare myself to face the worst, to fight patiently? With a wealth of twenty-five dollars I should not starve. I quickly sat down to plan my expenditure, including my food allowance, for the following weeks.

Car fare	60 cents
Newspapers	6
Bread	25
Butter	20
Beans	14
Milk	20
Sugar	7
Total	$1.52

Plus $1.00 for room rent, $2.52 per week, subject to change as soon as I should find work.

The next thing was to decide what to look for. I knew no trade, and the season on sweaters would not begin for some time. I bought a paper and looked through the advertisements. It was too late to go out to look for a job that day, so I sat at home, reading.

The next day I began to look for work. Day in, day out, I travelled the city from north to south, from east to west, in search of work. I answered all the advertisements, but in vain. I could find no job at dresses, because in the slack time no learners were taken. In general, learners found it hard to enter a trade. I tried straw hats—the papers were full of advertisements for workers in that trade—but I would have to pay twenty-five dollars and work for a month without pay in order to learn that trade. Flowers, corset-box making, everything I tried, and as the weeks passed, my courage lessened with each vanishing dollar.

And so more than a year had passed since I left home. Without English, with no relatives, I fought my battles bitterly. Now, on New Year's Eve, I had two dollars in my pocket, two dollars between me and starvation!

Tired, my head aching from the memories so vividly appearing before me, rushing so poignantly through my brain, I fell into restless sleep.

"WOMAN'S WORK" ON THE FRONTIER

Many women at work on farms did not even get counted by the census as "gainfully employed." Anna Howard Shaw, who later became one of the most remarkable of the early professional women (she was a medical doctor, a minister of the gospel, an enormously effective public speaker, and president of the Woman Suffrage Association), had some experience with "woman's work" on the frontier when she was a child.

The division of labor planned at the first council was that mother should do our sewing, and my older sisters, Eleanor and Mary, the housework, which was far from taxing, for of course we lived in the simplest manner. My brothers and I were to do the work out of doors, an arrangement that suited me very well, though at first, owing to our lack of experience, our activities were somewhat curtailed. It was too late in the season for plowing or planting, even if we had possessed anything with which to plow, and, moreover, our so-called "cleared" land was thick with sturdy tree stumps. Even during the second summer plowing was impossible; we could only plant potatoes and corn, and follow the most primitive method in doing even this. We took an ax, chopped up the sod, put the seed under it, and let the seed grow. The seed did grow, too—in the most gratifying and encouraging manner. Our green corn and potatoes were the best I have ever eaten. But for the present we lacked these luxuries.

We had, however, in their place, large quantities of wild fruit—

Anna Howard Shaw, The Story of a Pioneer (*New York: Harper & Brothers, 1915*), *pp. 32–33, 45. Copyright 1915 by Harper & Brothers; renewed 1943 by Lucy E. Anthony. Reprinted by permission of Harper & Row, Publishers, Inc.*

gooseberries, raspberries, and plums—which Harry and I gathered on the banks of our creek. Harry also became an expert fisherman. We had no hooks or lines, but he took wires from our hoop skirts and made snares at the ends of poles. My part of this work was to stand on a log and frighten the fish out of their holes by making horrible sounds, which I did with impassioned earnestness. When the fish hurried to the surface of the water to investigate the appalling noises they had heard, they were easily snared by our small boy, who was very proud of his ability to contribute in this way to the family table.

During our first winter we lived largely on cornmeal, making a little journey of twenty miles to the nearest mill to buy it; but even at that we were better off than our neighbors, for I remember one family in our region who for an entire winter lived solely on coarse-grained yellow turnips, gratefully changing their diet to leeks when these came in the spring.

Such furniture as we had we made ourselves. In addition to my mother's two chairs and the bunks which took the place of beds, James made a settle for the living room, as well as a table and several stools. At first we had our tree-cutting done for us, but we soon became expert in this gentle art, and I developed such skill that in later years, after father came, I used to stand with him and "heart" a log. . . .

When I was fifteen years old I was offered a situation as school-teacher. By this time the community was growing around us with the rapidity characteristic of these Western settlements, and we had nearer neighbors whose children needed instruction. I passed an examination before a school board consisting of three nervous and self-conscious men whose certificate I still hold, and I at once began my professional career on the modest salary of two dollars a week and my board. The school was four miles from my home, so I "boarded round" with the families of my pupils, staying two weeks in each place, and often walking from three to six miles a day to and from my little log schoolhouse in every kind of weather. During the first year I had about fourteen pupils, of varying ages, sizes, and temperaments, and there was hardly a book in the schoolroom except those I owned. One little girl, I remember, read from an almanac, while a second used a hymn book. . . .

MR. DOOLEY ON THE "NEW WOMAN"

Much of the discussion about women at work was very
solemn indeed, but Mr. Dooley, the Irish bartender created by
Finley Peter Dunne, took a somewhat lighthearted look at the
"new woman."

"Molly Donahue have up an' become a new woman!
"It's been a good thing f'r ol' man Donahue, though, Jawn. He
shtud ivrything that mortal man cud stand. He seen her appearin'
in th' road wearin' clothes that no lady shud wear an' ridin' a
bicycle; he was humiliated whin she demanded to vote; he put his
pride under his ar-rm an' ma-arched out iv th' house whin she committed assault-an'-batthry on th' piannah. But he's got to th' end
iv th' rope now. He was in here las' night, how-come-ye-so, with his
hat cocked over his eye an' a look iv risolution on his face; an' whin
he left me, he says, says he, 'Dooley,' he says, 'I'll conquir, or I'll
die,' he says.

"It's been comin' f'r months, but it on'y bust on Donahue las'
week. He'd come home at night tired out, an' afther supper he was
pullin' off his boots, whin Mollie an' th' mother begun talkin' about
th' rights iv females. ' 'Tis th' era iv th' new woman,' says Mollie.
'Ye're right,' says th' mother. 'What d'ye mean be the new woman?'
says Donahue, holdin' his boot in his hand. 'Th' new woman,' says
Mollie, ' 'll be free fr'm th' opprision iv man,' she says. 'She'll
wurruk out her own way, without help or hinderance,' she says.
'She'll wear what clothes she wants,' she says, 'an' she'll be no man's
slave,' she says. 'They'll be no such thing as givin' a girl in marredge
to a clown an' makin' her dipindant on his whims,' she says. 'Th'
women'll earn their own livin',' she says; 'an' mebbe,' she says, 'th'
men'll stay at home an' dredge in th' house wurruk,' she says. 'A-ho,'
says Donahue. 'An' that's th' new woman, is it?' he says. An' he
said no more that night.

"But th' nex' mornin' Mrs. Donahue an' Mollie come to his dure.
'Get up,' says Mrs. Donahue, 'an' bring in some coal,' she says. 'Ye
drowsy man, ye'll be late f'r ye'er wurruk.' 'Divvle th' bit iv coal

Finley Peter Dunne, Mr. Dooley in Peace and War *(Boston: Small and*
Maynard, 1899), pp. 136–40.

I'll fetch,' says Donahue. 'Go away an' lave me alone,' he says. 'Ye're inthruptin' me dreams.' 'What ails ye, man alive?' says Mrs. Donahue. 'Get up.' 'Go away,' says Donahue, 'an lave me slumber,' he says. 'Th' idee iv a couple iv big strong women like you makin' me wurruk f'r ye,' he says. 'Mollie 'll bring in th' coal,' he says. 'An' as f'r you, Honoria, ye'd best see what there is in th' cupboard an' put it in ye'er dinner-pail,' he says. 'I heerd th' first whistle blow a minyit ago,' he says; 'an' there's a pile iv slag at th' mills that has to be wheeled off befure th' sup'rintindint comes around,' he says. 'Ye know ye can't aford to lose ye're job with me in this dilicate condition,' he says. 'I'm going to sleep now,' he says. 'An', Mollie, do ye bring me in a cup iv cocoa an' a pooched igg at tin,' he says. 'I ixpect me music teacher about that time. We have to take a wallop out iv Wagner an' Bootoven befure noon.' 'Th' Lord save us fr'm harm,' says Mrs. Donahue. 'Th' man's clean crazy.' 'Divvle's th' bit,' says Donahue, wavin' his red flannel undhershirt in th' air. 'I'm the new man,' he says.

"Well, sir, Donahue said it flured thim complete. They didn't know what to say. Mollie was game, an' she fetched in th' coal; but Mrs. Donahue got nervous as eight o'clock come around. 'Ye're not goin' to stay in bed all day an' lose ye'er job,' she says. 'Th' 'ell with me job,' says Donahue. 'I'm not th' man to take wurruk whin they'se industhrees women with nawthin' to do,' he says. 'Show me th' pa-apers,' he says. 'I want to see where I can get an eighty-cint bonnet f'r two and a half.' He's that stubborn he'd've stayed in bed all day, but th' good woman weakened. 'Come,' she says, 'don't be foolish,' she says. 'Ye wudden't have th' ol' woman wurrukin 'in th' mills,' she says. ' 'Twas all a joke,' she says. 'Oh-ho, th' ol' woman!' he says. 'Th' ol' woman! Well, that's a horse iv another color,' he says. 'An' I don't mind tellin' ye th' mills is closed down today, Honoria.' So he dhressed himsilf an' wint out; an' says he to Mollie, he says: 'Miss Newwoman,' says he, 'ye may find wurruk enough around th' house,' he says. 'An', if ye have time, ye might paint th' stoop,' he says. 'Th' ol' man is goin' to take th' ol' woman down be Halsted Sthreet' an' blow himsilf f'r a new shawl f'r her.'

"An' he's been that proud iv th' victhry that he's been a reg'lar customer f'r a week."

WHEN WORK IS SCARCE

Books could be written about the effect of the Great Depression of 1929–40 on the lives of American women. One contemporary study tried to find out how unemployment had affected working women. Lorine Pruett was a sociologist who taught at several American colleges and universities and was herself an example of the new professional woman.

The chief conclusions to be derived from the experiences of many women out of work during the past years are very simple. Some of the women will withdraw more and more from ordinary social contacts, will make gestures toward jobs which are not really designed to succeed, and day by day will retreat into a dreary little world of their own. They will refuse to learn from their disasters, finding reasons to believe themselves unjustly treated, and come to regard others as malevolent creatures to whom they owe nothing, from whom they are justified in taking anything.

Such women huddle in hall bedrooms in New York, rooms a little stuffy, never quite free from the odor of stale food, or scuttle furtively to the bathroom and the corner cafeteria. Their eyes are slightly red and very wary, and they treasure for themselves some evidence of lost grandeur, some scarf or photograph or strange box which assures them that they are not what they seem. They are quick to take offense, full of pride and terror and an odd tenacity toward life, and their minds are sick.

Then much more numerous, apparently, are the women who have in part at least triumphed over their difficulties. The occasional woman is better off than before. Many of them have learned valuable lessons from the depression and are more responsible workers.

And a great many of them have learned a new kind of fear. They have been out of work for too long not to know fear for the new job. As a result they will probably demand less in the future; they will accept much that they do not like before they will give up the new job. This situation is true for men, too, who have had a long

Lorine Pruett, Women Workers Through the Depression *(New York: The Macmillan Company, 1934), pp. 45–46.*

struggle to get back to work. It raises serious questions as to whether such workers will not be particularly in danger of exploitation in the next few years.

THE DISADVANTAGE
OF BEING FEMALE AND BLACK

Within the whole range of women workers none suffered more under the multiple handicaps of inadequate training and discrimination than black women. Their difficulties were further compounded by the Depression, as was made clear in a government bulletin published in 1938.

One in every six women workers in America is a Negro, according to the lastest census figures—those of 1930. In all, nearly 2,000,000 Negro women were classed as gainful workers at that time. How many of these women now have jobs and how many are unemployed; where the employed women are working; how much they earn, and how their wages compare with those of white women workers: these are questions that have a direct bearing on the economic problems of today.

Though women in general have been discriminated against and exploited through limitation of their opportunities for employment, through long hours, low wages, and harmful working conditions, such hardships have fallen upon Negro women with double harshness. As the members of a new and inexperienced group arrive at the doors of industry, the jobs that open up to them ordinarily are those vacated by other workers who move on to more highly paid occupations. Negro women have formed such a new and inexperienced group in wage employment. To their lot, therefore, have fallen the more menial jobs, the lower-paid, the more hazardous —in general, the least agreeable and desirable. And one of the tragedies of the depression was the realization that the unsteady foothold Negro women had attained in even these jobs was lost when great numbers of unemployed workers from other fields clamored for employment.

Jean Collier Brown, The Negro Woman Worker, *Bulletin 165 of the Woman's Bureau (Washington, D.C.: Government Printing Office, 1938), pp. 1-4.*

Not very much is actually known about the economic position of Negro women today. The depression caused serious employment displacements that cannot be measured accurately. However, certain work problems of Negro women are outstanding and may be discussed with some measure of authority. To that end it may be well to discuss what is known concerning the general occupational position of Negro women; and further, something of each major occupational group as to numbers of workers, employment opportunities, hours, wages, and working conditions, and any other factors that may be of special importance.

OCCUPATIONAL STATUS

On the whole, most women, white or Negro, work for their living just as do men, not because they want to but because they must. The reason larger proportions of Negro than of white women work lies largely in the low scale of earnings of Negro men. In their pre–Civil War status it was the ability of Negro women to work that governed their market value. At the close of the Civil War a large proportion of all Negro women—married as well as single—were forced to engage in breadwinning activities. In 1930, at the time of the latest census, it was found still true that a larger proportion of Negro women than of white women were gainfully occupied. Practically two in five Negro women, in contrast to one in five white women, work for their living.

In pre–Civil War days the employment of the Negro woman was almost completely restricted to two fields where work is largely unskilled and heavy—agriculture and domestic service. Agriculture utilized the large majority of workers. In 1930 about nine in every ten Negro women still were engaged in farm work or in domestic and personal service, with more than two-thirds of them in domestic and personal service. The major occupational shift for Negro women has been, therefore, within these two large fields of employment. What occupational progress Negro women have made has been for the most part in connection with their entrance into the better-paid, better-standardized occupations in domestic and personal service. In addition, increases have been shown in the last twenty years in the professions and in clerical work. From 1910 to

1930 there was an increase of 33,000 Negro women in manufacturing, though a small decrease took place between 1920 and 1930. . . .

Unemployment. Today, eight years after that [1930] census, though there are no complete statistics on unemployment for the whole country, it is certain that the plight of Negro domestics since the beginning of the depression has been an exceedingly serious one. Certain scattered data such as follow are indicative of the situation as a whole.

In a comprehensive study of employment and unemployment in Louisville, Ky., conducted by the state Department of Labor in the spring of 1933, it was found that a little over one-half of the Negro women, in contrast to less than three-tenths of the white women, were without jobs. More than three-fourths of the Negro women wage earners in the survey depended on domestic and personal service for their livelihood, but the depression had thrown 56 percent of these out of work.

In a survey by the Federal Emergency Relief Administration of persons on relief in forty urban centers as of May 1, 1934, over two-thirds of the approximately 150,000 women who described their usual occupations in terms of servants and allied workers were Negro. For twenty-three northern and midwestern cities the difference in number between white and Negro women in this classification was not so great—54,000 Negro women as against 37,000 white women; but in the seventeen southern cities covered in the FERA report there were only 5,000 white women, as against 52,000 Negro women, classed as servants and allied workers.

Household service. So much for the unemployment of Negro domestic labor. But what about the working conditions of various types of domestic and personal service workers? The largest group, and the one concerning which there is the least definite information as to employment standards, is that of household workers. . . .

From common knowledge, and according to the few recent scattered studies that are available, low wages and long hours are characteristic of household service. In a survey of household employment in Lynchburg, Va., in the spring of 1937, the typical wage of the group covered—largely Negro workers—was $5 or $6 a week. Two cases were reported at $1.50 and one at $10, and there was one report of payment in the form of a house "on the lot" rent-free, and one of payment made only in clothing. The typical hours were seventy-two a week. There were sixteen reports of eighty to ninety hours and there was one report of a week of ninety-one hours.

A compilation of household employment data for the South in 1934, in which some twenty-six YWCA local associations cooperated, showed that the average weekly wage for Negro workers was $6.17 and the average workweek was sixty-six hours.

During the period of the National Recovery Administration a survey of household employment in thirty-three northern counties in Mississippi, conducted by the Joint Committee on National Recovery, showed that wages of Negro domestics usually amounted to less than $2 a week.

An informal investigation of household employment was made in the spring of 1937 by a Washington, D.C., committee representing women's organizations, by inquiries of both private and public employment agencies. The study showed that the general minimum weekly wage at which workers were placed was $5, and the average was from $7 to $10. The chief demands were for mothers' helpers at the $5 wage, and for general workers. The large majority of applicants were Negro women. Inadequate living and working conditions on the job were reported for many households. In a number of homes no bathing facilities were provided for the workers; too often the bed was found to consist of a cot in the living room or furnace room. Long hours and heavy work were characteristic of many jobs and the difficulty of managing children constituted another problem.

Laundresses and laundry operatives. The census makes a distinction between women laundresses who are self-employed, working in their own or their employers' homes, and operatives employed in commercial laundries. In 1930 there still were about 270,000 Negro women laundresses not in laundries, despite the rapid rise of power laundries in the decade from 1920 to 1930. There were nearly 50,000 Negro women laundry operatives.

Though employment conditions generally are better standardized and more favorable for women in commercial laundries than in private homes, the direct influence of home laundry work on the hour and wage standards set by the commercial laundry can be seen clearly. In a study of laundries by the Women's Bureau in 1935, bureau agents were told again and again that commercial laundries, especially in the South, were having a terrific struggle to compete with Negro washwomen. The following comments made by laundry employers, employment office officials, and other informed persons illustrate the conditions at that time:

> Since the depression, servants are required to do laundry as well as maid work; most of them get only $3 a week on the average.
> Greatest competition is colored washwomen. Will take a thirty-pound bundle for a dollar. Some of them do a week's washing for fifty cents.
> The washwoman charges only 60 to 75 percent of what the laundry charges for the same size bundle.
> The manager knew of a number of washwomen who were glad to get a day's work for carfare, lunch, and an old dress.

WE WOULD NEVER HAVE MADE IT
WITHOUT MOMMA

Woman's Bureau research told the story of black women one way. In his autobiography Dick Gregory makes the statistics come alive.

Like a lot of Negro kids, we never would have made it without our Momma. When there was no fatback to go with the beans, no socks to go with the shoes, no hope to go with tomorrow, she'd smile and say: "We ain't poor, we're just broke." Poor is a state of mind you never grow out of, but being broke is just a temporary condition. She always had a big smile, even when her legs and feet swelled from high blood pressure and she collapsed across the table with sugar diabetes. You have to smile twenty-four hours a day, Momma would say. If you walk through life showing the aggravation you've gone through, people will feel sorry for you, and they'll never respect you. She taught us that man has two ways out in life—laughing or crying. There's more hope in laughing. A man can fall down the stairs and lie there in such pain and horror that his own wife will collapse and faint at the sight. But if he can just hold back his pain for a minute she might be able to collect

Dick Gregory with Robert Lipsyte, Nigger: An Autobiography (*New York: E. P. Dutton & Co., Inc., 1964), pp. 39–43. Copyright © 1964 by Dick Gregory Enterprises, Inc. Reprinted by permission of E. P. Dutton & Co., Inc., and George Allen & Unwin Ltd.*

herself and call the doctor. It might mean the difference between his living to laugh again or dying there on the spot.

So you laugh, so you smile. Once a month the big gray relief truck would pull up in front of our house and Momma would flash that big smile and stretch out her hands. "Who else you know in this neighborhood gets this kind of service?" And we could all feel proud when the neighbors, folks who weren't on relief, folks who had Daddies in their houses, would come by the back porch for some of those hundred pounds of potatoes, for some sugar and flour and salty fish. We'd stand out there on the back porch and hand out the food like we were in charge of helping poor people, and then we'd take the food they brought us in return.

And Momma came home one hot summer day and found we'd been evicted, thrown out into the streetcar zone with all our orange-crate chairs and secondhand lamps. She flashed that big smile and dried our tears and bought some penny Kool-Aid. We stood out there and sold drinks to thirsty people coming off the streetcar, and we thought nobody knew we were kicked out— figured they thought we *wanted* to be there. And Momma went off to talk the landlord into letting us back in on credit.

But I wonder about my Momma sometimes, and all the other Negro mothers who got up at 6 A.M. to go to the white man's house with sacks over their shoes because it was so wet and cold. I wonder how they made it. They worked very hard for the man, they made his breakfast and they scrubbed his floors and they diapered his babies. They didn't have too much time for us.

I wonder about my Momma, who walked out of a white woman's clean house at midnight and came back to her own where the lights had been out for three months, and the pipes were frozen and the wind came in through the cracks. She'd have to make deals with the rats: leave some food out for them so they wouldn't gnaw on the doors or bite the babies. The roaches, they were just like part of the family.

I wonder how she felt telling those white kids she took care of to brush their teeth after they ate, to wash their hands after they peed. She could never tell her own kids because there wasn't soap or water back home.

I wonder how my Momma felt when we came home from school with a list of vitamins and pills and cod liver oils the school nurse said we had to have. Momma would cry all night, and then go out and spend most of the rent money for pills. A week later, the white man would come for his eighteen dollars rent and Momma would plead with him to wait until tomorrow. She had lost her pocketbook. The relief check was coming. The white folks had some money for her. Tomorrow. I'd be hiding in the coal closet because there was only supposed to be two kids in the flat, and I could hear the rent man curse my Momma and call her a liar. And when he finally went away, Momma put the sacks on her shoes and went off to the rich white folks' house to dress the rich white kids so their mother could take them to a special baby doctor.

Momma had to take us to Homer G. Phillips, the free hospital, the city hospital for Negroes. We'd stand on line and wait for hours, smiling and Uncle Tomming every time a doctor or a nurse passed by. We'd feel good when one of them smiled back and didn't look at us as though we were dirty and had no right coming down there. All the doctors and nurses at Homer G. Phillips were Negro, too.

I remember one time when a doctor in white walked up and said: "What's wrong with him?" as if he didn't believe that anything was.

Momma looked at me and looked at him and shook her head. "I sure don't know, Doctor, but he cried all night long. Held his stomach."

"Bring him in and get his damned clothes off."

I was so mad the way he was talking to my Momma that I bit down too hard on the thermometer. It broke in my mouth. The doctor slapped me across my face.

"Both of you go stand in the back of the line and wait your turn."

My Momma had to say: "I'm sorry, Doctor," and go to the back of the line. She had five other kids at home and she never knew when she'd have to bring another down to the City Hospital.

And those rich white folks Momma was so proud of. She'd sit around with the other women and they'd talk about how good their white folks were. They'd lie about how rich they were, what nice parties they gave, what good clothes they wore. And how they were going to be remembered in their white folks' wills. The next morning the white lady would say: "We're going on vacation for two months, Lucille, we won't be needing you until we get back." Damn. Two-month vacation without pay.

I wonder how my Momma stayed so good and beautiful in her soul when she worked seven days a week on swollen legs and feet, how she kept teaching us to smile and laugh when the house was dark and cold and she never knew when one of her hungry kids was going to ask about Daddy.

I wonder how she kept from teaching us hate when the social worker came around. She was a nasty bitch with a pinched face who said: "We have reason to suspect you are working, Miss Gregory, and you can be sure I'm going to check on you. We don't stand for welfare cheaters."

Momma, a welfare cheater. A criminal who couldn't stand to see her kids go hungry, or grow up in slums and end up mugging people in dark corners. I guess the system didn't want her to get off relief, the way it kept sending social workers around to be sure Momma wasn't trying to make things better.

I remember how that social worker would poke around the house, wrinkling her nose at the coal dust on the chilly linoleum floor, shaking her head at the bugs crawling over the dirty dishes in the sink. My Momma would have to stand there and make like she was too lazy to keep her own house clean. She could never let on that she spent all day cleaning another woman's house for two dollars and carfare. She would have to follow that nasty bitch around those drafty three rooms, keeping her fingers crossed that the telephone hidden in the closet wouldn't ring. Welfare cases weren't supposed to have telephones.

But Momma figured that some day the Gregory kids were going to get off North Taylor Street and into a world where they would have to compete with kids who grew up with telephones in their houses. She didn't want us to be at a disadvantage. She couldn't explain that to the social worker. And she couldn't explain that while she was out spoon-feeding somebody else's kids, she was worrying about her own kids, that she could rest her mind by picking up the telephone and calling us—to find out if we had bread for our baloney or baloney for our bread, to see if any of us had gotten run over by the streetcar while we played in the gutter, to make sure the house hadn't burnt down from the papers and magazines we stuffed in the stove when the coal ran out.

But sometimes when she called there would be no answer. Home was a place to be only when all other places were closed.

THE EFFECTS OF WAR

The depression threw large numbers of women out of work and made it harder for others to find jobs. The Second World War reversed all this and, as had been the case with all previous wars, it opened many new doors to women who were willing to step over traditional boundaries. "Rosie the Riveter," who took a job in a war plant to replace a man who had gone overseas and to help win the "battle of production," became a sort of folk heroine. In this selection one of these girls tells a little of what it was like.

Today I went on the night shift and I hope my iron constitution is as happy about it as I am. It makes normal living a little backward, but at least I'll have more time to sleep.

Now the schedule will go something like this, in case you're interested in the private life of a night worker: Sleep until 10 in the morning . . . work at the *Globe* until 2 in the afternoon, and then have an enormous hot dinner which would do credit to a soldier, a sailor, or a boy from the Marines . . . and then off to the factory, arriving just in time to punch in at 4 o'clock. Work until midnight . . . reach home at 1:30 in the morning, go to sleep at 1:31. It's the life of a fireman.

We bring our lunches, and have a supper period from 8 o'clock until a quarter of 9. But dinner at 8 is too long away, and most of us take a rest period at 6, and in 15 minutes manage to do away with a sandwich and orange. Tonight I thought the girls were joking when they said the regular supper period was at 8, so I finished all my lunch at 6 o'clock. They say it's a sign you're a freshman at this business.

Tonight I had a good job . . . it was to bore twenty holes in an aluminum disk which is part of one of the instruments we make. There are four drills . . . each of a different size . . . on the machine I used, and a metal box, called a fixture, into which you

Nell Giles, Punch In, Susie! *(New York: Harper & Brothers, 1943), pp. 41–43. Copyright, 1943, by Nell Giles. Reprinted by permission of Harper & Row, Publishers, Inc.*

place the disk to be drilled. The disk fits in just a certain way, and is marked with holes which indicate where you are to drill. The trick is to pull down the lever of the drill, which is spinning like mad, so that the drill goes into that one little hole, and doesn't hit the fixture.

There are about ten ways to break a drill, I've discovered, but one of the easiest is to snap it against the fixture. If the metal you are drilling is thick you must let the drill up several times during the process of making the hole so that the metal chips can come out. Otherwise the drill gets clogged and will break.

The people who have done this for some time can do hundreds of these disks and hardly seem to look at what they're doing. The average number of this certain one I did tonight with twenty holes to be drilled, is something like 166 in seven hours.

But there are other jobs which have a phenomenal speed rate. A boy across the table from me tonight did 700 disks in an hour! What he was doing is called "tapping," which means threading the hole so that a screw will fit in.

You would be amazed to know the number of processes involved in getting a piece of metal ready to be assembled. The holes are drilled, "burred" and then "tapped," if the metal is thick enough, so that the screw must actually be screwed in to fit tight.

On this floor we do nothing but machine work. On the floor above us, the girls wind the coils, and above that there is a clean and fascinating place where everything is put together and there are fifteen Army Air Corps inspectors to pass or reject the final product. Our own inspectors go over each part of the instrument with an eagle eye, and if the Army Air Corps men are any tougher than our own inspectors, they must eat nails for breakfast.

Naturally, the inspector's job is a vital one since it is his responsibility to see that each instrument which leaves our factory is 100 percent perfect. The methods of testing for perfection are so involved that I'll devote an article to that a little later.

Coming home from work so late at night is in a way like going to work early in the morning. The earth, and not the people, seems abnormally impressive. When you move about your business in the ordinary times of day, you never stop to look at the sky or remark on the freshness of the air.

THE LIFE OF A WORKING-CLASS WIFE

Patricia Cayo Sexton, a professor of educational psychology at New York university, contributed a revealing essay to a special supplement on "The American Female" published in 1962.

There is both the unique and the typical in all of us. Take myself for example: To begin with, I am a college professor (not too old a one but already mildly absent-minded), a sociologist, and a woman; a mixture which is a statistical improbability in itself.

Moreover, I am an ex-schoolteacher, radio commentator, waitress, movie usher, barmaid, typist, switchboard operator, factory worker, full-time union steward (UAW), and a long list of other things I've never bothered or dared to list on job applications. Also, though I've never worked at it for pay, I must admit I'm a bit of a fanatic.

What is typical about me is that I am "working-class" through and through. And because I am in this sense a "type" I feel entitled to write impressionistically, though not sociologically, about the working-class woman.

My credentials are:

A mother who is now and has been for almost twenty years a sewer (mechanized seamstress, that is) in the Ford Highland Park plant, Detroit. She is now remarried to a handy man in the same department.

A father, deceased during the Great Depression, who was a welder and maintenance man in the same Ford plant, drawing his pay in Ford scrip some of the time. Before that, during his vigorous years, he was a poet, an embroiderer, and a professional boxer (K.O. Cayo: middleweight and one-time title contender): a tough, taciturn, uneducated man but, also, a deeply learned and handsome one who bore the visible scars of the ring (a tin ear and a broken nose), plus the deeper scars of a rigorous French-Canadian-Duluth youth.

Patricia Cayo Sexton, "Speaking for the Working-Class Wife," Harper's Magazine *(October 1962): 129–32. Reprinted by permission of the author.*

I was born and raised in a working-class family in working-class
towns (Duluth and Detroit), and my sense of kinship with workers,
however marginal my present status may be, is complete. I now
see that my fanatic loyalty to workers is hooked up with family
affection, but that doesn't change the feeling a bit. I am unalterably
working-class: by inheritance, association, and personal preference.
I'm not sure what accounts for the strength of this bond. Friends
of mine, many of them in the academic world, have shed working-
class ties the way reptiles shed last year's skin. The skin doesn't
fit when you're on the way up and it's wiser to be rid of it if you
want to move fast. I've tried, but I can't do it.

My forebears were Basques, a fiercely proud, egalitarian breed
who by tradition oppose central authority and who were major
supporters of the anti-Fascist resistance in Spain. A queer people
these Basques, an ancient race preserved almost intact (having
resisted Roman, Visigoth, and Frankish conquest) with a non-Aryan
language resembling no other in the world.

My own tribe in this hemisphere were woodsmen and trappers
in Gaspé, Quebec, a magnificently rugged spot regarded even by
the Indians as the end of the world. Now, when I think of these
odd people, way up there in the wilderness, I feel a strong pull of
kinship. Perhaps this brings me closer to the working-class woman
whom I brashly claim to typify.

Working-class women are, it appears to me, the most deprived
large group in our society and the most estranged from what is
vital in the world. Because of this, the worker's wife is better off
by far, in my view, when she gets out of the house and takes on
a job and independence. Working is a way for her to break out,
to live, to come into her own. Of course it's not an easy path; it
means facing the usual female dilemma and the pull of dual roles,
wife and worker. It means time-clock routines and a heavier load
of responsibilities. But it's worth it. Jobs mean freedom, independence, excitement for women. More than that, jobs mean
equality, or a route to it.

Breaking Out of the Cage

True, the House is often a refuge for women. But escape from
life leaves no life at all. Women comply—because husband, chil-

dren, church, and state seem to expect it—but there is usually at least a wistful longing to break out and a well-founded suspicion that they are missing something important.

Working-class women are easily trapped; most lack the courage, the know-how to break through. They stay in their cages, quiet and desperate, working out unhappy compromises with their spouses, very often battling for position or giving in and taking a beating.

The brightest days of my mother's life were her first days of work—as a school janitress—during the Depression. The "glamour" wore bare but it still beat staying home. The job offered new hope, new routines, and a regular pay check. It was the beginning of a new life of labor, hard labor, but it offered her what it offers every worker—warm and varied associations with other workers, and the ironic sense that, despite low-man status, she was after all her own boss with her own source of income.

I am not using these pleasant thoughts simply to cover the shame, guilt, and anger I feel because my mother works at least twice as hard as I do. I know she is better off working, and she does too. The conditions of her labor—I do what I can about, which is not much. Mostly I feel inertly ashamed that our places are not reversed. Younger, with the energy and stamina for much harder labor, I nonetheless lead a life of relative leisure, free to do what I want, go where I choose, with enough salable skills to face unemployment without paralyzing fear, and with a present earning capacity of about twice my mother's . . . and a three-month scholar's holiday to boot.

My mother works a tight eight-hour day, with half-an-hour for lunch; the routine is so demanding that she has nothing left for herself. As fatiguing as the job is (her index finger is swollen to more than twice its natural size from tugging on the "decking" and her eyes are similarly injured from staring eight hours a day at a moving needle) . . . yet she does all her own housework when she leaves the shop, including floor scrubbing, window washing, and other heavy duties.

She has always done all of her own housework, even when she had two kids plus a full-time job—and with shockingly little help from the two kids, I'm sorry to recall. Superwoman? Perhaps . . . but there are thousands like her—working-class women who carry back-breaking loads and who somehow call up the inner strength to move on without stumbling.

Nowadays she still rises at 4:30 A.M., returns home at 3:30, does her housework, eats, naps, reads the evening paper, takes in a little TV, if weather permits, a customary drive down the main street of town, and retires at ten o'clock. That's it and has been for almost twenty years. She gets two weeks' vacation but rarely goes anywhere. Still, life is better than before.

My mother's only point of contact with the outside world used to be through my father and yet she complained that he did not talk to her enough. Of course, he was a taciturn man, but few workers talk much to their wives. They have little to say about their jobs (the same routine), and little common meeting ground. Unlike most middle-class men, they have interests, tastes, experiences often very different from their wives'. So there is little rapport; the man would rather talk with his barroom buddies about baseball, leaving the stay-at-home wife starved for adult talk.

A job gives a woman something to talk about and someone to talk to; it makes it easier to stay alive and alert, to keep up with husband and children; it gives her organized purpose. More than this, it helps her face advancing years, when children scatter, life changes, and the nest egg somehow doesn't hatch.

Chances are fifty-fifty, in the words of a medical report, that the aged woman in the U.S. will end up "impoverished, in dismal, pathetic financial straits." With a backlog of work and savings behind her, she is less likely to die on the poor farm. The non-working widow is now the most desperate of all senior citizens; almost half get less than $50 a month from Social Security. My mother, who will retire in a few years on Social Security, plus union pension, will get about $200 a month. She also has some savings—not much, for she is a rash spender, but some. Though she has no hobbies or special interests, and will find retirement difficult, it will be easier than for the pauperized widow.

Working-class women ask very little, and usually get it. Like others of her class, at least in past generations, my mother was conditioned by parental authority and religious training to self-denial, self-effacement, and sacrifice (O Lord, I am unworthy). It was always part of the unspoken scheme of things in our household that her loss would be our profit, and that she would sink so we could swim, but without any of the aura of martyrdom some women acquire.

It was the accepted thing, the salmon battling upstream, spawning, and perishing, a part of nature's design. So extreme is her abnegation that my mother can never accept a gift with genuine pleasure; the gift is returned to the store, to the giver, or left on the shelf unused. When she gave something to her children it was part of a guilt payment, guilt about poverty and unfilled obligations. Also of course it was the natural reflex of a charitable woman who had learned her place in the world and submitted to her fate without any spoken protests.

But it was not the guilt of the middle-class woman, fearful she is neglecting her children. The working-class woman spends too much time with her children, works too hard, and is too untouched by soothsaying psychologists to feel guilt of this kind. In my own house I was never left in the care of baby-sitters or left behind while my parents vacationed. But then my parents never traveled, never went anywhere. Neglect would have been too expensive a luxury.

"Play Something Gayer"

Like others of her background, my mother has never voluntarily joined any organized group, outside her union. Once a church member, she did not so much leave, as slide out from under; now she feels guilty but not especially repentant. She does not give or go to teas. She does not play games, in or out of doors, except an occasional hand of poker or pinochle. She actively dislikes sports, concerts, opera, ballet, theatre. (Classical music she often finds too sad: "Play something gayer.") She likes occasional films and is an astute critic, with an X-ray eye for detecting sham, pretense, phoniness, and stupidity. Living across from an Art Theatre now, she has even developed a taste for good foreign films; but she is still taken in now and then by extravaganzas of the De Mille kind.

She is skeptical and suspicious, yet the most innocent of believers, childlike in fact, with a soft shell that has not protected her well from life's blows. Her only cushion against pain is the simple knowledge that, whatever happens, you must somehow make the best of things . . . and above all, you must never show that it hurts, ask for help, or burden others with your problems. The same kind of simple persistence in my own temperament, the quiet

refusal to be pushed under and submerged got me out of the shop
and into the university.

A pooh-pooher of most varieties of human activity, my mother
has only one mild enthusiasm: She plays the horses. She's not a
bug, but she knows the track and who's running and uses a book
occasionally when she can't get to the track. The horses and the
numbers are popular with workers. No one comes out ahead but
it's a thrill and a wild chance to win big.

The drabness of real life seems to affect taste. If your life is
exciting you are likely to decorate in stark Danish and wear simple
unadorned black classics. But in my mother's house there is glitter
—a dazzling wall clock that bongs every half-hour, an oversized,
wood-inlaid painting of Chinese dancers (à la Coney Island), painted
figurines of bongo players, and a giant Buddha perched atop the
TV. In her clothes my mother prefers bright reds to black. She
will choose the flashy fakes over subdued pearls, big beads over
smaller ones, and three strands over one. Size, quantity, and glitter
always count. Her car is an orange and white Mercury (now in its
declining years), and her hair is of rather similar hues—it all seems
somehow gayer that way.

My mother has never palled around with the girls or been any
part of the coffee klatch circuit. In my youth the local bar was
the substitute, still is. Only now the drinking rounds are slimmed
down by pressures of work and age to Saturday night outings.
Even this is falling off as TV takes over and fills up the living-
room with the "company" that was once found only in bars.
Working-class adults of my acquaintance were nearly all heavy
and steady drinkers.

The bar is a social club for many workers. Unlike middle-class
groups, workers rarely "entertain" at home, except for relatives
now and then. At our house, we never had parties or planned
gatherings; it would have been as unthinkable as joining a country
club. Even now "entertaining" is an awkward job for me.

All planning was foreign to our life. How plan, when all future
time, beginning the next moment, was so uncertain and on the
whole more threatening than promising? Only those with bright
past and futures will take premature steps into the unknown. For
the others, it is something you face when you get into it and not
a moment before. . . .

The working-class woman is trained to accept what's given her without complaint. She has almost no sense of control over her own destiny or power over the course of events in the outer world. What she does usually reflects what others want her to do, for above all she aims to please and besides she seldom knows what she wants for herself. She has been taught to follow, not to lead, to listen, not to talk, and she soon learns to accept herself as an inferior being, one who take orders, whose opinion is worth little. She is almost strictly a non-complainer, except to her husband. . . .

THE EFFORT TO INVADE THE PROFESSIONS

While many women worked for pay because they had to eat, others were anxious to try their talents in jobs which had been for the most part confined to men. In colonial days women had pleaded their own lawsuits, provided much of the medical care for families and neighbors, and taught the children. By the nineteenth century most of the lawyers, doctors, preachers and a good number of the teachers were men. As early as the 1840s a few hardy women aspired to enter these professions, which meant that they needed professional education. Elizabeth Blackwell, for example, had to combat immense prejudice before she could secure medical training and begin to practice medicine. Antoinette Brown, later to be Miss Blackwell's sister-in-law, had been among the early women students at Oberlin College, and there she conceived the desire to become an ordained minister. In a letter to Lucy Stone[1] (who was also later to marry a Blackwell brother) she described long discussions with one of her professors who thought it appropriate for women to speak in public meetings but who said that the idea of a woman's becoming an ordained minister was "perfectly absurd." She had tried to refute his arguments from the scripture, but her professor thought women should use theology only in "their sphere." Yet he was more liberal than most men, for among all the ministers she knew not one would even discuss the subject.

1. The complete text of this undated letter from Antoinette Brown to Lucy Stone is in the Blackwell Papers, Schlesinger Library, Radcliffe College, Cambridge, Mass.

WORK AS PERSONAL EXPRESSION

Charlotte Perkins Gilman's Women and Economics *went through at least seven editions and was said to have been the bible of the Vassar girls at the turn of the century. She thought women needed to do more than housework if they were to be "fully developed human beings."*

The change is more perceptible among women than among men, because of the longer survival of more primitive phases of family life in them. One of its most noticeable features is the demand in women not only for their own money, but for their own work for the sake of personal expression. Those who object to women's working on the ground that they should not compete with men or be forced to struggle for existence look only at work as a means of earning money. They should remember that human labor is an exercise of faculty, without which we should cease to be human; that to do and to make not only gives deep pleasure, but is indispensable to healthy growth. Few girls today fail to manifest some signs of this desire for individual expression. It is not only in the classes who are forced to it: even among the rich we find this same stirring of normal race energy. To carve in wood, to hammer brass, to do "art dressmaking," to raise mushrooms in the cellar—our girls are all wanting to do something individually. It is a most healthy state, and marks the development of race distinction in women with a corresponding lowering of sex distinction to its normal place.

In body and brain, wherever she touches life, woman is changing gloriously from the mere creature of sex, all her race functions held in abeyance, to the fully developed human being, none the less true woman for being more truly human. What alarms and displeases us in seeing these things is our funny misconception that race functions are masculine. Much effort is wasted in showing that women will become "unsexed" and "masculine" by assuming these human duties.

Charlotte Perkins Gilman, Women and Economics *(Boston: Small and Maynard, 1898), pp. 157–58.*

PROGRESS BY 1900

*At the turn of the century Carrie Chapman Catt summed
up the progress women had made in the professions in the
nineteenth century.*

The real contest centred about the three learned professions,
since the opposition there combined the prejudice against the
woman worker, the prejudice against financial independence for
women, and the scepticism concerning woman's intellectual ability.
This portion of the history of the industrial evolution of women
offers the truest measure of changed conditions. In the early years
of the century the higher vocations were entirely beyond the reach
of women. Three distinct and overpowering obstacles stood in the
way:

1. The belief, practically universal, that the minds of women
were wholly incapable of mastering a college education, and still
less the training required by a learned profession; and that their
physical strength was insufficient to endure the strain of so long a
period of close study. (Oberlin College was opened in 1833, but no
women were graduated until 1841.)

2. The belief, quite as universal, that if a woman should receive
the necessary professional training, no patrons would reward her,
and her preparation, in consequence, would represent a loss of
time and money.

3. The popular belief that any woman who would seek to enter
a profession must of necessity be masculine, "unsexed," indelicate,
and unworthy of public esteem.

The first profession opened to women was medicine. [Mrs. Catt
here gave a detailed account of the trials of the Blackwell sisters in
securing a medical education.]

For many years medical practice of a desirable kind was difficult
for women physicians to secure. Patients came at first chiefly from
the poor. Women who should, according to theory, have been the
best patrons of their pioneer sisters, were influenced by popular
opinion and offered neither support nor encouragement. The preju-

"Women in the Industries and Professions" in The Nineteenth Century: A
Review of Progress (*New York: G. P. Putnam & Sons, 1901*), *pp. 193, 198–201.*

dice which was overwhelming in 1840 has not been entirely elimi-
nated; yet at the close of the century women are admitted to the
medical societies of the United States and England, are accepted
in consultation with men physicians, and the practice of many of
them is large, successful, and lucrative. At the close of the century
there are in the United States and Canada forty-nine medical
colleges admitting women, nine being separate women's schools.
Seven hundred graduated women physicians are reported as practising in Russia, several hundred are practising in the British
Empire and colonies; there are women physicians in all countries
of Europe, in China, Japan, Persia, India, and Egypt; and it is
estimated that some ten thousand graduated women physicians are
practising in the United States.

In 1850, Antoinette Brown was graduated from Oberlin, and
immediately made application to enter the theological department.
The president did his utmost to dissuade her, but failing in this
he was forced to admit her, owing to the exceedingly liberal character of the college charter. She pursued the entire course, and,
despite the fact that faculty and trustees continued their disapproval of her presence there, was graduated with honour in 1853.
However, to guard against further applicants the Oberlin charter
was so amended as to prevent other women from entering the
theological school, and her name was not printed in the list of
graduates until forty years after her graduation. Miss Brown was,
shortly after her graduation, ordained by a Congregational church
in New Jersey. At about the same date, the Universalist Church
ordained the Rev. Olympia Brown. Some denominations did not
require a diploma from a theological school as a qualification, and
on that account offered easier means of entrance than others; but
this advantage, open to men, offered no encouragement to women,
since it was offset by the overpowering belief that the ministry
of women was contrary to God's Word. There are now some
eighteen denominations, including Friends and the Salvation Army
(which do not require ordination), that permit women to preach.
Several hundred women are occupying regular pulpits. Those
churches whose government is determined by large representative
bodies, such as the Methodist Episcopal Conference and the Presby-
terian Assembly, have never granted ordination to women. The
denominations in which ordination may be secured at the request
of a single congregation are those in which women ministers are

most numerous. The so-called liberal denominations—Unitarian and Universalist—have ordained the largest number of women in proportion to their total membership. Among the churches which have ordained women are the Unitarian, Universalist, Congregational, Baptist, Free Baptist, Methodist Protestant, Free Methodist, Christian, and United Brethren.

The law was the last profession to admit women, and it will doubtless be the last to concede fair opportunity. Yet the opposition is disappearing, the number of women lawyers is increasing, and sooner or later the law, too, will unquestionably offer equal chances to women. Permission to practise law in nearly all countries can be obtained only by decree of a court. In several states, courts threw off the responsibility of passing upon the application of women candidates by the decision that a special act of the legislature must first be secured, making women eligible to the profession of law. In 1869, Belle Mansfield was admitted to the bar in Iowa; that same year, Myra Bradwell made application for admission to the bar in Illinois, and was refused. She appealed to the Supreme Court of the United States, which decided that each state must determine the question for itself. Several women are now practising law in Illinois, and many states have admitted them to practice; but in each state a special effort had to be made to secure the right for the first candidate. Western states presented little difficulty, but eastern states withheld the privilege longer. Several hundred women have since been graduated from law schools, and many are engaged in honourable and lucrative practice. Women have been graduated in law in several foreign countries, but although efforts to secure admission to the bar have been made in Italy, Belgium, Switzerland, and Russia, they have thus far been in vain.

Although woman in the "learned professions" still has difficulties to overcome in addition to those which confront man, it is evident that these are growing fewer every year. Basing one's judgment upon the rapidity with which conditions have changed in the last fifty years, a prophecy may be ventured with safety that in a few years the professional woman and professional man will stand before the world with equal chances of success or failure. The constantly increasing demand of women for work, the gradual decrease of prejudice against the woman worker, and the improved standard of qualification have opened nearly all occupations to women, and all the professions, learned and otherwise, within the last fifty years.

No occupation illustrates more clearly the immensity of the changes wrought than teaching. As early as 1789, women were beginning to teach in country districts, in the summer months, when the schools were small and mainly confined to girls. The wages were much below those paid to men, even for summer schools, while winter schools, attended by boys, were considered quite beyond the capacity of women. The change of opinion has been slow but decided. In some states four-fifths of the teachers are women, while for the whole United States more than half the teachers are women. Most southern states still employ more men than women teachers, but northern and western states employ more women than men. In 1880 there were 100,000 women teachers in the public schools of the United States; in 1890, 236,912. The highest positions are usually reserved for men, and there is still unequal pay for equal work in most states. Many professorships in colleges and universities, representing every phase of scholarship, from ancient languages to modern science, and from literature to engineering, are held by women. The profession of teacher is also open to women in foreign countries, though they are mainly confined to positions in primary and intermediate schools. There, as in the United States, teaching was the first profession to admit women. The universities of Sweden, Italy, and Switzerland have employed women in responsible positions as instructors.

ARE WOMEN THEIR OWN WORST ENEMIES?

As more and more women came into the labor force it became apparent that they were not distributed over the whole spectrum of jobs but were largely concentrated in lower-paid, less-influential positions. In 1970 only 15 percent of all women workers were "professional and technical workers" and only 4 percent were "managers, officials, and proprietors." Many peo-

Lorine Pruett, "Why Women Fail" in Samuel D. Schmalhausen and V. F. Calverton, Woman's Coming of Age (New York: Horace Liveright, 1931), pp. 252–53. Copyright renewed 1959 by Liveright Publishing Corp. Reprinted by permission of Liveright Publishing Corp.

*ple blamed this on prejudice, but occasionally an observer
suggested that women's own attitudes also invited their second-
class positions. Lorine Pruett, whose work on women workers
in the depression has already been quoted, looked at this
question in the early thirties.*

. . . The businessman begins to feel himself a success when he
can have a secretary. Some girl with a pencil in her hand must be
audience to his prancing, must be consolation to his vanity when
it is wounded, must be his conscience in social matters, his protection from annoyance and his excuse when things go wrong. The
stenographer is wife and mother, child and mistress, with this advantage that she may always be left at the end of the day and
discharged at the end of the week. When he thinks of it the employer is apt to wax rhetorical and say that this is Miss So and So,
who runs me while I run the business. It used to be the hand that
rocks the cradle rules the world, now we seem to hear more from
our masculine sentimentalists about Miss So and So who runs me
while I run the business. Few men appear to know that they require their stenographers to be at least a little in love with them
(although employers have been quoted advising this), but many
of them rely upon this just the same. The woman worker may
never have learned shorthand and she may type with one finger,
but if she does not watch out business will catch her and make her
a stenographer at heart. One of the enlightened woman's agencies
has been known to advise girls to conceal their knowledge of ste-
nography, but this is not enough; they need to get a change of
heart. Many an assistant chief and many a woman executive remains always in the stenographic attitude toward some man in the
organisation, while he never quite ceases to expect her to remind
him to wear his rubbers and to look after his cough.

The stenographic attitude is a part of the general attitude of
being a woman and leading a contingent life. Most women still lead
contingent lives. It is not quite nice for them to be greedy and
grasping for themselves, but they can be shameless for another—a
man or a child. Great numbers of them prefer to work through
another person and to find their own joys and compensations in
the success of another. This is not so self-sacrificing; generally it
appears to be the easier way. They still see their own success as
involved in a close personal relation, and often if they keep the

relation close enough they seem to forget the necessity of making it a success. Thus the hordes of discontented wives who, ceasing to appear admirable or desirable to their husbands, continue to demand money and prestige and attention because they are wives; thus the defrauded mothers whose children seek only to escape them while they clamour that the child bring back increasing tribute from that world with which the mothers have never dared to cope. We are only recently becoming aware of the evils of contingent living. Bitterness and frustration threaten any woman who seeks to find all her satisfactions in the efforts of another person, and disaster threatens the relation that involves this demand.

Contingent living. Not the firm satisfaction of a task performed as well as it may be, but the rewards of pleasing some other person. If women could get over the necessity of being pleasing, one very great obstacle to their success would be removed. We teach them in their cradles to be pleasing, and when they grow up find that they have learned their lesson too well. The graces and virtues inculcated in the growing girl belong to a noncompetitive existence, the luxurious ornamentation for America's only leisure class. Knowing how to please is a valuable asset in getting a husband, although not necessarily in keeping one, and is of use at tea parties and in some of the minor jobs for which women show such a predilection.

WHY SEEK A PROFESSION?

Inez Haynes Irwin was a journalist, writer, and militant suffragist. In 1926 she explained why.

. . . Away back in the early stirrings of my young-girl thinking I became definitely conscious of a growing impatience with the woman's lot. From the moment I was able to think for myself—and I suppose I could number on the fingers of one hand the women I have met in a lifetime who have not agreed with me—I regretted bitterly that I had not been born a man. Like all young things I yearned for romance and adventure. It was not, however, a girl's kind of romance and adventure that I wanted, but a man's. I wanted to run away to sea, to take tramping trips across the coun-

Inez Haynes Irwin, "These Modern Women: The Making of a Militant," Nation 123 (December 1, 1926): 554–55.

try, to go on voyages of discovery and exploration, to try my hand at a dozen different trades and occupations. I wanted to be a sailor, a soldier. I wanted to go to prize fights; to frequent barrooms; even barber shops and smoking rooms seemed to offer a brisk, salty taste of life. I could not have been more than fourteen when I realized that the monotony and the soullessness of the lives of the women I knew absolutely appalled me.

This was, understand, life in the middle class. These were, understand, women without private means or without the capacity for earning money for themselves.

I saw that most of them enjoyed one brief period of budding and another of flowering; the romance periods of young love and early marriage. After that—my heart sank as I contemplated the picture. All about me I saw lovely young things marrying, producing an annual baby, taking care of too many children in the intervals of running their houses. It seemed to me that early they degenerated into one of two types: the fretful, thin, frail, ugly scold or the good-natured, fat, slatternly slut.

As I look back on those years, the midday Sunday dinner seemed in some curious way to symbolize everything that I hated and dreaded about the life of the middle-class woman. That plethoric meal—the huge roast, the blood pouring out of it as the man of the house carved; the many vegetables, all steaming; the heavy pudding. And when the meal was finished—the table a shambles that positively made me shudder—the smooth replete retreat of the men to their cushioned chairs, their Sunday papers, their vacuous nap, while the women removed all vestiges of the horror. Sunday-noon dinners! They set a scar upon my soul. I still shudder when I think of them.

A profound horror of the woman's life filled me. Nothing terrified me so much as the thought of marriage and childbearing. Marriages seemed to me, at least so far as women were concerned, the cruelest of traps. Yet most women married and all seemed to want to marry. Those who remained single often changed into something more repellent than those charmless drudges. I made all kinds of resolutions against matrimony. All the time, though, I was helplessly asking myself, how was I going to fight it—when I so loved companionship?

One way, I decided, was not to let myself get caught in any of those pretty meshes which threaten young womanhood. I made a vow that I would never sew, embroider, crochet, knit—especially would I never learn to cook. I made a vow that if those things had to be done, I would earn the money to pay for them. I married, but I kept my vow. I have always paid for them. Even in a young marriage, when income was very limited, I went without clothes to keep a maid. And although I happen to be extremely domestic in that I must have a home and much prefer to stay in it, I have always managed that the work of that home should be done by someone else, and that my clothes should be made outside it.

Through all this spiritual turmoil there had been developing within me a desire to write. And during all these years, I was making a tentative experiment with the august business of reflecting the life about me. Ultimately my first short story was accepted; more short stories; a book; more books. Except for three or four years, my mature life has been economically independent. I hope to be economically independent the rest of my days. When I look back on my fifty-odd years of life on this planet, I wonder what was the real inception of my desire to stand alone—fighting ancestry; liberal influences; discussion-ridden youth? Perhaps it was those Sunday dinners!

DIFFICULTIES OF PROFESSIONAL WOMEN

Alice Hamilton, who virtually invented the field of industrial medicine, had decided early that she wanted a career. To her own amazement in 1918 she was appointed to the faculty of Harvard Medical School. In her autobiography, written in the 1940s, she reminisced about some of the attitudes she and other women doctors encountered.

A few years after my arrival Ruth Tunnicliffe joined the group and proved herself a really eminent bacteriologist, with as brilliant success as a woman can have in that field. This means that she could be a member of any scientific society she chose, could read papers and publish them, and win the respect of her colleagues quite as well as if she were a man, but she could not hope to gain a position of any importance in a medical school. I remember

Alice Hamilton, Exploring the Dangerous Trades (*Boston: Little, Brown and Company, 1943*), pp. 95, 252–53. Copyright 1942, 1943 by Alice Hamilton. Reprinted by permission of Atlantic-Little, Brown and Co.

taking her to see the head of a department of pathology in a medical school where the chair of bacteriology was vacant. The pathologist received her with cordiality and respect and together they discussed their work for some time, then he spoke of the vacancy in the medical school and went over with her the qualifications of the different candidates who were being considered. Had she been a man she would almost certainly have been chosen, but it never occurred to him even to consider her. . . .

During the fall of 1918, on one of my trips to Washington, Dr. David Edsall, dean of Harvard Medical School and one of my advisers on the National Research Council's committee, had asked me if I would come to Boston in April and give three Cutter lectures to the medical school. My astonishment can be imagined, for Harvard was then—and still is—the stronghold of masculinity against the inroads of women, who elsewhere were encroaching so alarmingly. Of course I was both pleased and proud to accept and I worked very hard on those three lectures, but before I left for Boston the Cutter lectures had come to seem almost unexciting compared to the much greater event of my appointment to Harvard as assistant professor of industrial medicine.

Harvard had not changed her attitude toward women students in any way, yet here she was putting a woman on the faculty. It seemed incredible at the time, but later on I came to understand it. The medical school faculty, which was more liberal in this respect than the corporation, planned to develop the teaching of preventive medicine and public health more extensively than ever before. Industrial medicine had become a much more important branch during the war years, but it still had not attracted men, and I was really about the only candidate available. I was told that the corporation was far from enthusiastic over this breaking away from tradition, and that one member had sworn roundly over it. "But then," said my informant, "you know, he always swears." Another member had asked anxiously if I would insist on my right to use the Harvard Club, which at that time had no ladies' entrance, and did not admit even members' wives. One of my backers had promised them I never would nor would I demand my quota of football tickets, and of course I assured him that I should never think of doing either. Nor did I embarrass the faculty by marching in the commencement procession and sitting on the platform, though each year I received a printed invitation to do so.

At the bottom of the page would be the warning that "under no circumstances may a woman sit on the platform," which seemed a bit tactless, but I was sure it was not intentional.

EVEN POETS ARE NOT EXEMPT FROM PREJUDICE

Perhaps writing poetry is not a profession, and certainly women have written for centuries. Nevertheless Edna St. Vincent Millay encountered a strange situation in 1937 when New York University conferred an honorary degree upon her.

To the Secretary of New York University

One Fifth Avenue
May 22, 1937

. . . Having answered your questions, I come now to that aspect of your commencement activities regarding which, I said, I felt impelled to speak.

I received from Mr. Chase, your chancellor, in a letter dated April 26, the information that New York University wished to confer upon me on the occasion of its commencement on the ninth of June, the honourary degree of Doctor of Humane Letters. In the same letter Mr. Chase informed me that Mrs. Chase would be pleased to receive me as guest of honour at a dinner given for a small group of ladies at the chancellor's house on the evening before commencement.

I answered at once, accepting the award of the degree with happiness and pride, and the invitation to dinner with pleasure.

In your letter, dated May 4, I was told for the first time that on the evening of the dinner given in honour of me by the chancellor's wife, a quite separate dinner is to be given at the Waldorf-Astoria in honour of the other recipients of honourary degrees, that is, the male recipients.

On an occasion, then, on which I shall be present solely for reasons of scholarship, I am, solely for reasons of sex, to be excluded from the company and the conversation of my fellow-doctors.

Letters of Edna St. Vincent Millay (*New York: Harper & Row, 1954*), *pp. 290–91. Copyright 1954 by Norma Millay Ellis. Reprinted by permission of Norma Millay Ellis.*

Had I known this in time, I should have declined not only Mrs. Chase's invitation to dinner, but also, had it appeared that my declining this invitation might cause Mrs. Chase embarrassment, the honour of receiving the degree as well.

It is too late to do either now, without making myself troublesome to everybody concerned, which I do not wish to do. I shall attend Mrs. Chase's dinner with pleasure; and I shall receive the degree the following morning with a satisfaction only slightly tempered by the consciousness of the discrimination against me of the night before.

Mrs. Chase should be the last, I think, to be offended by my attitude. I register this objection not for myself personally, but for all women.

I hope that in future years many women may know the pride, as I shall know it on the ninth of June, of receiving an honourary degree from your distinguished university.

I beg of you, and of the eminent council whose representative you are, that I may be the last woman so honoured, to be required to swallow from the very cup of this honour, the gall of this humiliation.

Very sincerely yours,
Edna St. Vincent Millay.

THE PRESENT SCENE

The Woman's Bureau of the United States Department of Labor pays close attention to working women and their needs. Two recent "fact sheets" give some sense of the present status of women in the labor force, and in professional and technical positions.

PROFILE OF THE WOMAN WORKER:
FIFTY YEARS OF PROGRESS

Now	1920
AGE	
39 years old.	28 years old.

U.S. Department of Labor, Wage and Labor Standard Administration, Women's Bureau 70-34, and 69-60.

MARITAL STATUS

Married and living with her hus-   Single.
band.

OCCUPATION

Most likely to be a clerical worker.

Other large numbers of women are
service workers outside the home,
factory workers or other operatives, and professional or technical workers.

May be working in any one of 479
individual occupations.

Most likely to be factory worker
or other operative.

Other large numbers of women were
clerical workers, private household workers, and farm workers.

Occupational choice extremely limited.

EDUCATIONAL ATTAINMENT

High school graduate with some college or post-secondary-school education.

Only one out of five 17-year-olds in
the population graduated from
high school.

LABOR FORCE PARTICIPATION

Almost half of all women 18 to 64
years of age in the population
are workers (49 percent).

Most apt to be working at ages 20
to 24 (56 percent in April, 1969).

Participation in the labor force
drops off at age 25 and rises again
at age 35 to a second peak of 54
percent at ages 45 to 54.

Can expect to work 24 to 31 more
years at age 35.

Less than one-fourth of all women
20 to 64 years of age in the population were workers (23 percent).

Most apt to be working at ages 20
to 24 (38 percent in January,
1920).

Participation in the labor force
dropped off at age 25, decreased
steadily with age, and was 18 percent at ages 45 to 54.

Less than 1 out of every 5 women
35 to 64 years of age was in the
labor force (18 percent).

FACT SHEET ON WOMEN IN TECHNICAL
AND PROFESSIONAL POSITIONS

An increasing demand for skilled and highly trained workers has
accompanied the rapid growth and changing technology of our
economy. Women have shared in the rising number of professional
and technical workers. Prior to World War II, women employed in
professional and technical positions numbered about 1.6 million.
In the first nine months of 1968 they averaged 3.8 million. How-

ever, men have moved into these jobs at an even faster pace. As a result, women held only 37 percent of all professional and technical positions in the first nine months of 1968, as compared with 45 percent in 1940. . . .

Despite the increased diversification in women's professional employment, women continue to hold a disproportionately small share of positions in the leading professions. Although traditionally women have made up a large part of the teacher corps, only 22 percent of the faculty and other professional staff in institutions of higher education were women in 1964 (the most recent date for which comparable figures are available). This is a considerably smaller proportion than they were in 1940 (28 percent), 1930 (27 percent), or 1920 (26 percent), and only slightly above their proportion in 1910 (20 percent). Similarly there has been a sharp decline in the proportion of women among all secondary school teachers—46 percent in 1967 as compared with 57 percent in 1950.

Although women are heavily represented in the health fields, in 1967 only 7 percent of physicians were women. Similarly women had only a token representation among scientists (8 percent), lawyers (3 percent), and engineers (1 percent). Moreover, a survey by the *Harvard Business Review* states that "the barriers [to the employment of women in management positions] are so great that there is scarcely anything to study." [1]

1. *Harvard Business Review* (March–April, 1965), p. 8.

Chapter 3

Education

When Lucretia Mott surveyed "the degraded condition" of her fellow women in the mid-nineteenth century, she stressed the need for "education and elevation" to improve their plight. This emphasis on education was a prominent motif in feminists' writings. An articulate sixteenth-century woman had protested that man permitted woman "only enough education to tell her husband's bed from that of another." At the end of the eighteenth century, Mary Wollstonecraft's classic *Vindication of the Rights of Woman* begged for more emphasis on the development of women's minds and less on cultivating their charms. Emma Willard, who induced a male college student to teach her day by day what he learned at Middlebury, tried as early as 1819 to persuade the New York State Legislature that it should provide for the education of girls. The legislature was unmoved, but Mrs. Willard's private seminary at Troy, New York, pioneered in serious intellectual training for women. In the 1830s Mary Lyon opened Mt. Holyoke Seminary and Oberlin admitted a few women. After the Civil War, Vassar College and then Smith, Wellesley, Bryn Mawr, and the "Harvard Annex" (which would become Radcliffe College) aspired to give girls an education equal to any in the country.

In the beginning there were so few girls prepared for college that these institutions had to organize preparatory departments. Nor did women's colleges win wide public approval. It was seriously suggested that education was physically detrimental to women, that they would get brain fever, and that—anyway—their minds would not be able to cope with hard subjects. Other critics claimed that college women did not marry and therefore the education of women would lead to race suicide. Even so, one after another of the mid-western colleges admitted women.

As time went by and nobody died of brain fever, as girls in the coeducational colleges made better grades than their male colleagues, and as women college graduates began to distinguish themselves in the world, the number of college women increased steadily. Some women went on to advanced training, and as early as 1900 there were a number of women Ph.D.'s, many of them on the faculties of the women's colleges.

During the years before 1920 it seemed that the number of women taking advanced degrees would continue to grow with each decade, but at some point there was a turnabout. Although 4.8 percent of the law degrees in 1930 were taken by women, in 1950 the percentage was only 3.7. In 1930 more than 5 percent of the degrees in theology went to women, but by 1950 this had dropped to 1.5 percent. In other fields the percentage of women increased in that twenty years—from 4.6 to 5.2 percent of medical degrees, for example—but the changes were not impressive.

It may be that the 1960s witnessed the beginning of another turnabout and that the next decade will see a new surge of women into advanced training and into the professions. The whole question of education is, of course, closely allied to that of work, as well as to that of marriage.

A COED'S LIFE

Lucy Stone was raised on a New England farm, and since she had to earn her own money to go to college, she was twenty-five before she could afford to enroll at Oberlin. Her father did not approve of college education for women, so for the first years she was entirely on her own. Then he relented. Her daughter told the story.

In her third year, Father Stone's objections to a collegiate education for girls yielded to his respect for Lucy's courage, and to the affection which, under his rough exterior, he really felt for his children. He wrote to her on January 11, 1845:

Alice Stone Blackwell, Lucy Stone (*Boston: Little, Brown and Company, 1930*), *pp. 52–53.*

Lucy: The first thing you will want to know, after hearing that we are all well, will be about money. When you wrote that you had to get up at two o'clock to study your lesson, it made me think of the old tanyard where I had to get up at one and two o'clock. I little thought then that I should have children, or a child, that would have to do the same; not the same work, but perhaps as hard. I had to work late and early. I was hardly able to live; and you have been under the same inconvenience, as far as money is concerned. Let this suffice. There will be no trouble about money; you can have what you will need, without studying nights, or working for eight cents an hour.

I pay the postage on all letters that are sent and received, so pay no more postage.

Your Father Stone.

We do not know for which of her activities Lucy had been getting eight cents an hour. Perhaps it was for teaching in the colored school.

Lucy's third year was therefore easier financially, and she could devote more time to study. She wrote to her father and mother:

I want to tell you how I spend my time, so that you can think of me, and know each hour of the day what I am doing. I rise at five o'clock, and am busy until six taking care of my room and my person. At six we go to breakfast, which, with family worship, lasts until seven. Then I go and recite Latin until eight; from eight to nine recite Greek; from nine till ten, study algebra; from ten till eleven, hear a class recite arithmetic; from eleven to twelve, recite algebra; from twelve to one, dinner, and an exercise in the sitting room which all the ladies are required to attend. From one to two, hear a class recite arithmetic; from two to five, I study; five to six we have prayers in the chapel, and then supper. We study in the evening. These are the duties of every day except Monday, which is washing day. In the afternoon of Monday, from three to four, I attend composition class. In addition to what is done during the other days, we have, every Tuesday, to go to the Music Hall and hear a lecture from some one of the Ladies' Board of Managers—this from three to four o'clock.

THE BEGINNING OF COEDUCATION

Oberlin College had admitted a few women to the "full liter-ary course" in 1837. The college historian recounted the reaction to coeducation.

As the years went on Oberlinites became increasingly enthusiastic about "joint education," and it became an important part of the Oberlin Gospel. In 1851 it was officially reported that the results of the system were "cheering, beyond the most sanguine expectations." "The same teachers educate six hundred young gentlemen and young ladies at an expense to the public less than in most colleges is incurred in educating two hundred young men. The female pupils enjoy privileges for mental culture of a higher order than are enjoyed by ladies, perhaps in any other one school in the world. The mutual social and moral influence of the sexes has been highly salutary." Six years later Professor T. B. Hudson wrote to the *Independent:*

> The joint education of the sexes has been here attended by the best results. . . . The manners of both sexes are improved by proper association. Better order prevails in all departments. Sickly sentimentalism is checked. A quiet and healthy emulation is supplied to each sex by the presence of the other in the same classes. Meanwhile, the ladies are educated to be *women,* and not *men.*

In 1862, it was still a source of great pride. A statement in the *Oberlin Evangelist* described the system in glowing terms.

> Brothers and sisters are here on common platform of opportunities and facilities for education. They meet in the recitation room and at the table. Under wise social regulations, this system is proved to be fraught with many and great benefits, and liable to but few incidental evils. It enkindles emulation; puts each sex upon its best behavior; almost entirely expels from college those mean trickish exploits which so frequently deprave monastic college society, and develops in college all those humanizing, elevating influences which God provided for in the well-ordered association of the sexes together! [1]

Robert Fletcher, History of Oberlin College *(Oberlin: Oberlin College, 1943), vol. 1, pp. 383–85. Reprinted by permission of Oberlin College.*

1. *Oberlin Evangelist,* Dec. 3, 1851; Oct. 8, 1862; and the *Independent,* Aug. 7, 1856; Jan. 22, 1857.

The students seem to have been equally well satisfied. One young man wrote to an intercollegiate publication in 1860:

> Brothers in the monastic colleges we pity you, but we think there is hope, if not for you, of your successors. The day of deliverance dawns. . . . Women are to be educated because we choose civilization rather than barbarism. Of course in the ages when women were practically regarded as soulless, there could be no joint education. Man was educated alone because there was nobody else to be educated. The old institutions of learning were not organized on such a basis that women could be admitted into them. Hence if women were to be educated at all, seminaries must be built for them. But when the civilized world comes to adjust itself properly to the new phase of human progress, the education of woman, the sexes will be educated together. . . . It is our happy experience, of a quarter of a century's growth, that it is better for both sexes to travel together along the paths of science. Womanhood becomes more beautiful, and manhood more strong and elevated, as they are brought out side by side in harmonious contrast. The principle, that it is not good for man or woman to be alone, is older than any monastic seminary of learning. Separate from each other, the sexes cannot be educated in the best and highest sense.[2]

He prophesied more truly than he or his readers could have guessed:

> We read in the signs of the times, that in the next age the maiden shall, with her brother, con the classic page, and with him woo the muses in their sacred haunts. Be cheered by this promise of better things; God's plan as shown by the common nature, the likeness of himself which has impressed on man and woman, must succeed. God meant the joint education of the sexes. So it shall be. Our grand-children will wonder why it was not always so.

Even John Morgan, who, in 1835, wrote to Theodore Weld: "The mixing of young men and women together in the same institution strikes me as not at all judicious," was converted, and in 1872 bantered President Mark Hopkins on the failure of Williams to adopt coeducation. "I suppose," he wrote, "Williams is bound to be exclusive of ladies—a great mistake I think. But it may not last forever." [3]

2. "Oberlin College" in the *University Quarterly*, II (Oct., 1860), 372–73.
3. Morgan to Theodore Weld, June 13, 1835 (Weld MSS), and Morgan to Mark Hopkins, Sept. 12, 1872 (Morgan-Hopkins MSS).

Already, by 1867, several other American colleges had adopted "joint education." Two years before, Sophia Jex-Blake, the first British woman physician and a distinguished feminist, had written after a visit to Oberlin: "Whatever shortcomings or errors may be recorded against Oberlin, it should ever be remembered in her favor that she took the initiative before all the world in opening a college career to women." [4] In the next generation the propriety of college education for women was to become practically universally recognized in the United States, and, under the name of co-education, the system of educating the sexes together was to conquer a great part of the American college world, even long established men's colleges in the East trembling in the balance.

OBJECTIONS

Oberlin's growing enthusiasm for coeducation was not entirely typical. At Wisconsin the first women were admitted immediately after the Civil War, but the men were not enthusiastic.

James L. High, a distinguished alumnus of 1864, has testified to the feeling of the men students in his time:

The feeling of hostility was exceedingly intense and bitter. As I now recollect the entire body of students were without exception opposed to the admission of the young ladies, and the anathemas heaped upon the regents were loud and deep. Some of the students left for other colleges, and more of us were restrained only by impecuniosity from following their example. During the remaining year of my own college life the feeling of intense and bitter indignation caused by the change continued almost unabated.

Helen R. Olin, The Women of a State University *(New York: G. P. Putnam's Sons, 1909), pp. 101–2. Reprinted by permission of the publisher.*

4. Sophia Jex-Blake, *A Visit to Some American Schools and Colleges* (New York, 1867), p. 47, and the *Dictionary of National Biography, Twentieth Century,* 1912–21. On the later history of coeducation see [Fletcher], pp. 904–9.

AN EARLY COLLEGE GIRL

Jane Addams enrolled at Rockford Seminary in 1877 wishing she could go to Smith, but obedient to her father's desire to keep her close to home. A year after she graduated, partly due to her own efforts, Rockford became a degree-granting college. In her autobiography she described life among those early college women, including an interesting experiment with drugs.

As my three older sisters had already attended the seminary at Rockford, of which my father was trustee, without any question I entered there at seventeen, with such meager preparation in Latin and algebra as the village school had afforded. . . .

The school at Rockford in 1877 had not changed its name from seminary to college, although it numbered, on its faculty and among its alumnæ, college women who were most eager that this should be done, and who really accomplished it during the next five years. The school was one of the earliest efforts for women's higher education in the Mississippi Valley, and from the beginning was called "The Mount Holyoke of the West." It reflected much of the missionary spirit of that pioneer institution, and the proportion of missionaries among its early graduates was almost as large as Mount Holyoke's own. In addition there had been thrown about the founders of the early western school the glamour of frontier privations, and the first students, conscious of the heroic self-sacrifice made in their behalf, felt that each minute of the time thus dearly bought must be conscientiously used. This inevitably fostered an atmosphere of intensity, a fever of preparation which continued long after the direct making of it had ceased, and which the later girls accepted, as they did the campus and the buildings, without knowing that it could have been otherwise.

There was, moreover, always present in the school a larger or smaller group of girls who consciously accepted this heritage and persistently endeavored to fulfill its obligation. We worked in those early years as if we really believed the portentous statement from

Jane Addams, Twenty Years at Hull House *(New York: The Macmillan Company, 1910), pp. 43–48. Copyright 1910 by The Macmillan Company; renewed 1938 by James W. Linn. Reprinted by permission of the publisher.*

Aristotle which we found quoted in Boswell's Johnson and with which we illuminated the wall of the room occupied by our Chess Club; it remained there for months, solely out of reverence, let us hope, for the two ponderous names associated with it; at least I have enough confidence in human nature to assert that we never really believed that "There is the same difference between the learned and the unlearned as there is between the living and the dead." We were also too fond of quoting Carlyle to the effect, " 'Tis not to taste sweet things, but to do noble and true things that the poorest son of Adam dimly longs."

As I attempt to reconstruct the spirit of my contemporary group by looking over many documents, I find nothing more amusing than a plaint registered against life's indistinctness, which I imagine more or less reflected the sentiments of all of us. At any rate here it is for the entertainment of the reader if not for his edification: "So much of our time is spent in preparation, so much in routine, and so much in sleep, we find it difficult to have any experience at all." We did not, however, tamely accept such a state of affairs, for we made various and restless attempts to break through this dull obtuseness.

At one time five of us tried to understand De Quincey's marvelous "Dreams" more sympathetically, by drugging ourselves with opium. We solemnly consumed small white powders at intervals during an entire long holiday, but no mental reorientation took place, and the suspense and excitement did not even permit us to grow sleepy. About four o'clock on the weird afternoon, the young teacher whom we had been obliged to take into our confidence, grew alarmed over the whole performance, took away our De Quincey and all the remaining powders, administered an emetic to each of the five aspirants for sympathetic understanding of all human experience, and sent us to our separate rooms with a stern command to appear at family worship after supper "whether we were able to or not."

Whenever we had chances to write, we took, of course, large themes, usually from the Greek because they were the most stirring to the imagination. The Greek oration I gave at our Junior Exhibition was written with infinite pains and taken to the Greek professor in Beloit College that there might be no mistakes, even after the Rockford College teacher and the most scholarly clergyman in town had both passed upon it. The oration upon Bellerophon and his successful fight with the Minotaur, contended that social evils could only be overcome by him who soared above them into idealism, as Bellerophon mounted upon the winged horse Pegasus, had slain the earthy dragon.

There were practically no Economics taught in women's colleges —at least in the fresh-water ones—thirty years ago, although we painstakingly studied "Mental" and "Moral" Philosophy, which, though far from dry in the classroom, became the subject of more spirited discussion outside, and gave us a clew for animated rummaging in the little college library. Of course we read a great deal of Ruskin and Browning, and liked the most abstruse parts the best; but like the famous gentleman who talked prose without knowing it, we never dreamed of connecting them with our philosophy. My genuine interest was history, partly because of a superior teacher, and partly because my father had always insisted upon a certain amount of historic reading ever since he had paid me, as a little girl, five cents a "Life" for each Plutarch hero I could intelligently report to him, and twenty-five cents for every volume of Irving's "Life of Washington."

When we started for the long vacations, a little group of five would vow that during the summer we would read all of Motley's "Dutch Republic" or, more ambitious still, all of Gibbon's "Decline and Fall of the Roman Empire." When we returned at the opening of school and three of us announced we had finished the latter, each became skeptical of the other two. We fell upon each other with a sort of rough-and-tumble examination, in which no quarter was given or received; but the suspicion was finally removed that *any* one had skipped. We took for a class motto the early Saxon word for lady, translated into breadgiver, and we took for our class color the poppy, because poppies grew among the wheat, as if Nature knew that wherever there was hunger that needed food there would be pain that needed relief. We must have found the sentiment in a book somewhere, but we used it so much that it finally seemed like an idea of our own, although of course none of us had ever seen a European field, the only page upon which Nature has written this particular message.

That this group of ardent girls who discussed everything under the sun with such unabated interest, did not take it all out in talk, may be demonstrated by the fact that one of the class who married a missionary founded a very successful school in Japan for the children of the English and Americans living there; another of the class became a medical missionary to Korea, and because of her successful treatment of the Queen, was made court physician at a time when the opening was considered of importance in the diplomatic as well as in the missionary world; still another became an unusually skilled teacher of the blind; and one of them a pioneer librarian in that early effort to bring "books to the people."

A SUCCESSFUL WOMAN GRADUATE

Some of the first generation of college women embarked upon careers with spectacular success. Alice Freeman Palmer was president of Wellesley College at the age of twenty-six. Her husband, in his biography of her, quoted the remarks of the president of Harvard.

In speaking of Mrs. Palmer just after her death President Eliot said:

As we look back on the chief events of her too short career, the first thing that strikes us is its originality at every stage; she was in the best sense a pioneer all through her life. When she went to the University of Michigan as a student, she was one of a small band of young women, venturing with motives of intellectual ambition into a state university which had just been opened to women. At twenty-two years of age she was already principal of a high school in Michigan. At twenty-four she took a professorship of history in a new college for women where all the officers and teachers were women— a pioneer work indeed. At twenty-six she became president of that novel college, at a time when its worth had not yet been demonstrated. Indeed its policy was then held by many to be of doubtful soundness, and its financial future extremely difficult. What courage and devotion these successive acts required! Her work at Wellesley was creation, not imitation; and it was work done in the face of doubts, criticisms, and prophecies of evil.

George Herbert Palmer, Alice Freeman Palmer (Boston: Houghton Mifflin, 1908), p. 118. Reprinted by permission of the publisher.

WHAT DID THEY DO LATER?

In 1895 a writer in Forum *tried to sum up the experience of the first thirty years of Vassar College, suggesting some of the social implications of the increasing educational opportunity. What became of students when they left college?*

Vassar College reached its thirtieth birthday in September, 1895. Its brief existence practically covers the whole period of advanced education for women. Vassar opened its doors in September, 1865; Smith and Wellesley were established ten years later; Bryn Mawr, ten years later still; and the chief coeducational universities—Boston, Cornell, Michigan, and others—date from the neighborhood of 1870. Woman's opportunities for degree-taking are too numerous and too widely known to be even recounted at the present time; but there is a matter of kindred and greater interest about which almost no information has been collected. This is the subsequent career of the graduates. What becomes of the students after leaving college? What is the probable future of the girls who are now marching in battalions to our different educational institutions?

From the "Vassar General Catalogue," the "Alumnae Register," and the "Vassar Miscellany" (the college monthly) it is possible to gather tolerably complete information about the occupations of a thousand and more women who have received the degree of A.B. As Vassar is the oldest of the woman's colleges, and as these institutions have many more points of likeness than of unlikeness, its record may be taken as broadly typical of others.

The scientific student will at once see the difficulty of reaching exact conclusions. In the first place it is impossible to write the history of a living institution, especially of one so young as a woman's college. Again, it is beyond human power to get absolutely correct data for any census. Figures will always lie, no matter how carefully percentages are deduced. . . .

Vassar College has graduated twenty-nine classes, containing 1,182 members. As the class of '95, numbering 100, has made no record of any sort, it is obviously unfair to include it for statistical purposes;

Frances Abbott, "A Generation of College Women," The Forum *20 (November 1895): 377–80.*

hence the following computations will be based upon the total of 1,082 graduates, embracing all the classes between '67 and '94, inclusive, and including all alumnae who have been graduated one year or more.

The first question everybody is impatient to ask is, Do college women marry? . . . The record to date is this: Of 1,082 alumnae, 409 have married—a trifle less than 38 percent of the whole. As the "Miscellany" reports marriages every month, this percentage will be inaccurate before even another class has been graduated. A truer proportion may be found by taking the records of some of the earlier classes. The first class ('67) numbered four members: of these, three have married—75 percent. The class of '68 had twenty-five members: fifteen of these—or 60 percent—have annexed another name to that on their college diploma. Of the thirty-four members of '69, there are twenty-one married, or not quite 62 percent. The class of '70 presents nearly the same record: of the thirty-four members, twenty-two are married, or, as Miss Coffin of '70, a gifted artist, stated at the last alumnae luncheon: "Our matrons—in our class two-thirds of the whole number—have allayed the terrors of man lest he be left a forlorn bachelor wandering at the foot of the mountains of science and art, while woman, in her maiden robes, disappears from sight in the clouds of the summit." The last of these four classes has just celebrated its quarter-centennial. According to Mr. Charles Francis Adams, by the time a man has been twenty-five years out of college he has either failed or won in the battle of life. Assuming that a woman's occupation and prospects would be settled by that time, it may be stated that, in the first four classes of Vassar, sixty-one of the ninety-seven members—or about 63 percent—have married: a little less than two-thirds of the whole number. A college woman's chances of marriage, then, are about two to one: but even this will not do for an absolute statement; for, as matrimony can be entered upon at a greater age than almost any other profession, it is quite possible that the semicentennial of these classes may show an increased percentage in that direction. The average age of students upon graduating from Vassar is twenty-two years and some months. The late Maria Mitchell used to say, "Vassar girls marry late, but they marry well." Let us hope that time may not disprove her observations.

The time-honored profession of teaching ranks next to matrimony in engaging the attention of Vassar women. Of 1,082 graduates,

408—or 37.6 percent—are recorded as teachers. Some of these have taught only two or three years; perhaps less than half the number have made the profession a life work. Upon referring to the records of the first four classes we find but eighteen out of the ninety-seven members—or about 18.33 percent—now engaged in teaching. Many Vassar women have attained high rank in the educational profession. Vassar has furnished professors and instructors to Vassar, Smith, and Wellesley Colleges; an instructor to the Massachusetts Institute of Technology; instructors to several coeducational colleges; a dean to Barnard College; and principals and teachers to normal and high schools and to academies. In private-school work Vassar's influence has been large. Within the last few years the colleges have transformed the girls' private schools of this country, and much of this result is due to Vassar women, many of whom now control schools of their own.

Next in number to those who have engaged in imparting knowledge stands the group of women who have gone on acquiring knowledge for themselves. . . . The graduate record of Vassar to June, 1895, is as follows: fifty have received the degree of A.M.; eight have received the degree of Ph.D. (five of them from Yale); three, the degree of S.B. (Institute of Technology); two, that of LL.B.; and one, that of LL.D.—sixty-four in all. As far as can be ascertained, twenty-two are at present studying for advanced degrees. There is one student at each of the foreign universities at Heidelberg, Leipsic, Göttingen, Geneva, Dresden, and Brussels; and in our own country, Radcliffe, Yale, and the University of Chicago each claims several students. Four Vassar women also hold fellowships at the University of Chicago. Many other graduates have pursued special studies for longer or shorter periods at American and foreign universities. If we count in those who have pursued advanced courses of a strictly professional nature, we must add the physicians. There are twenty-five who have taken the degree of M.D. There are seven more who are now studying medicine at the Johns Hopkins and New York medical colleges, and at Chicago and Michigan universities. The general statement can then be made that eighty-nine graduates have taken the degrees of A.M., Ph.D., M.D., S.B., LL.B., and LL.D., and that twenty-nine are now pursuing advanced studies with that end in view. This is a total of 118, or nearly one-ninth of the entire number of Vassar alumnae.

Literary work ranks next in order. Forty-seven graduates (not including writers of scientific papers, who are classed by themselves), have furnished matter for the printing press. Nearly every magazine and review in this country, and some in England, and most of the prominent American daily and weekly papers, have published contributions from Vassar women. The forty-seven workers are divided as follows: twenty-four write for magazines and newspapers; six write for newspapers alone; there are five regular journalists; four authors of novels and children's books; four editors of papers; two editors of collections of poetry; and two authors of books on physical training. If Vassar has not yet startled the world with a genius "On Fame's eternall beadroll worthie to be fyled," she has at least contributed something to cultivated contemporary thought.

The medical profession has already been mentioned. Of the twenty-five graduates who have taken the degree of M.D., probably most are practicing physicians, though in some cases the additional title of MA has kept the married doctors from practicing outside their own homes. Seven medical students are reported. It seems rather strange that Vassar graduates are not more largely represented in the profession of medicine, which offers to women such wide opportunities for usefulness and comparatively large pecuniary returns. The only explanation that I can suggest is that women who have a decided bent for medicine do not seem to have the time or the money for a college course. In looking over the catalogues of woman's medical colleges, one finds the A.B.'s in a noticeable minority.

The sixth department of activity includes teachers who give other than book instruction. Under this head I have grouped eight teachers of music, two of painting, three of physical culture, two of industrial work, and one in an institution for the blind—sixteen in all.

The authors of scientific papers occupy the seventh place in point of numbers, but they include some graduates of the first distinction. The writers are twelve in all. Mrs. Christine Ladd-Franklin ('69), who has been a fellow at Johns Hopkins University and has received the degree of LL.D., is a phenomenal mathematician, and her papers on such subjects as the Pascal Hexegram, Methods of Determining the Horopter, the Algebra of Logic, etc., have appeared in the most advanced scientific periodicals and in the publications of Johns Hopkins University. Mrs. Ellen Swallow-Richards ('70), who properly belongs under the list of chemists, has published much in the line of chemical and mineralogical investigation. Mrs. Annie Howes-Barus ('74) did an important work in collecting the Health Statistics of Alumnae, which dealt the final blow to the old theory that a college education is injurious to a girl's health. Mrs. Barus is now investigating the Development of Children. Dr. Mary Sherwood ('83), who took her degree at the University of Zürich, and is now resident gynecologist at the Johns Hopkins Hospital, has had contributions in the reports of that institution—the only ones from a woman's pen. Miss Margaretta Palmer ('87), who completed the definitive orbit of Maria Mitchell's comet, has had papers printed in the "Transactions" of Yale Observatory; and Miss Ida Welt ('91), a young chemist of great promise, has had Researches on Dissymmetrical Hydrocarbons published by the Academy of Science of France.

IS IT SAFE TO SEND GIRLS TO COLLEGE?

Though this impressive record had already been compiled, in 1895 the doubting men were still numerous. In 1908 one of the nation's leading psychologists published a fat book on Adolescence, which contained a long chapter on the education of women. M. Carey Thomas, the militant president of Bryn Mawr said later of this chapter: "I . . . never chanced again upon a book that seemed to me so to degrade me in my womanhood as the seventh and seventeenth chapters of women and women's education in President Stanley Hall's Adolescence." Hall was not alone, however, in thinking that woman's peculiar constitution meant that she must be treated with the greatest care if her capacity for motherhood were not to be damaged by a college education.

First, the ideal institution for the training of girls from twelve or thirteen on into the twenties, when the period most favorable to motherhood begins, should be in the country in the midst of hills, the climbing of which is the best stimulus for heart and lungs, and tends to mental elevation and breadth of view. There should be water for boating, bathing, and skating, aquaria and aquatic life; gardens both for kitchen vegetables and horticulture;

G. *Stanley Hall,* Adolescence *(New York: D. Appleton and Co., 1904), vol. 2, pp. 636–40.*

forests for their seclusion and religious awe; good roads, walks, and paths that tempt to walking and wheeling; playgrounds and space for golf and tennis, with large covered but unheated space favorable for recreations in weather really too bad for out-of-door life and for those indisposed; and plenty of nooks that permit each to be alone with nature, for this develops inwardness, poise, and character, yet not too great remoteness from the city for a wise utilization of its advantages at intervals. All that can be called environment is even more important for girls than boys, significant as it is for the latter.

The first aim, which should dominate every item, pedagogic method and matter, should be health—a momentous word that looms up beside holiness, to which it is etymologically akin. . . .

Sleep should be regular, with a fixed retiring hour and curfew, on plain beds in rooms of scrupulous neatness reserved chiefly for it with every precaution for quiet, and, if possible, with windows more or less open the year round, and, like other rooms, never overheated. Bathing in moderation, and especially dress and toilet should be almost raised to fine arts and objects of constant suggestion. Each student should have three rooms, for bath, sleep, and study, respectively, and be responsible for their care, with every encouragement for expressing individual tastes, but with an all-dominant idea of simplicity, convenience, refinement, and elegance, without luxury. . . .

Exercise comes after regimen, of which it is a special form. . . .

Manners, a word too often relegated to the past as savoring of the primness of the ancient dame school or female seminary, are really minor or sometimes major morals. They can express everything in the whole range of the impulsive or emotional life. . . .

Another principle should be to broaden by retarding; to keep the purely mental back and by every method to bring the intuitions to the front; appeals to tact and taste should be incessant; a purely intellectual man is no doubt biologically a deformity, but a purely intellectual woman is far more so. Bookishness is probably a bad sign in a girl; it suggests artificiality, pedantry, the lugging of dead knowledge. Mere learning is not the ideal, and prodigies of scholarship are always morbid. The rule should be to keep nothing that is not to become practical; to open no brain tracts which are not to be highways for the daily traffic of thought and conduct; not to overburden the soul with the impedimenta of libraries and records

of what is afar off in time or zest, and always to follow truly the
guidance of normal and spontaneous interests wisely interpreted.

WHY ARE THERE NO WOMAN GENIUSES?

*One of the perennial arguments against spending money
to educate women was the assertion that there had never been
a woman genius—a strange position, but common. Anna
Garlin Spencer, in a book published in 1912, attacked this
argument head-on.*

The failure of women to produce genius of the first rank in most
of the supreme forms of human effort has been used to block the
way of all women of talent and ambition for intellectual achievement in a manner that would be amusingly absurd were it not so
monstrously unjust and socially harmful. A few ambitious girls in
the middle of the nineteenth century in Boston, the Athens of
America, want to go to high school. The board of education answers them, in effect: Produce a Michael Angelo or a Plato and
you shall have a chance to learn a bit of mathematics, history and
literature. A few women of marked inclination toward the healing
art want a chance to study in a medical school and learn facts and
methods in a hospital. Go to! the managing officials in substance
reply: Where is your great surgeon; what supreme contribution
has any woman ever made to our science? A group of earnest students beg admission to college and show good preparation gained
by hard struggle with adverse conditions. You can't come in, the
trustees respond, until you produce a Shakespeare or a Milton. The
demand that women shall show the highest fruit of specialized
talent and widest range of learning before they have had the general opportunity for a common-school education is hardly worthy
of the sex that prides itself upon its logic. In point of fact no one,
neither the man who denies woman a proper human soul nor the
woman who claims "superiority" for her sex, can have any actual
basis for accurate answer to the question, Can a woman become a
genius of the first class? Nobody can know unless women in general

Anna Garlin Spencer, Woman's Share in Social Culture, *2nd ed.* (Philadelphia:
J. B. Lippincott, 1925), *pp. 50–51; 81–83.* (First edition, 1912). Copyright, 1925,
by J. B. Lippincott Company. Reprinted by permission of the publisher.

shall have equal opportunity with men in education, in vocational choice, and in social welcome of their best intellectual work for a number of generations. So far women have suffered so many disabilities in the circumstances of their lives, in their lack of training in what Buckle calls "that preposterous system called their education," in their segregation from all the higher intellectual comradeship, in the personal and family and social hindrances to their mental growth and expression, that not even women themselves, still less men, can have an adequate idea of their possibilities of achievement. Nothing therefore is more foolish than to try to decide a priori the limits of a woman's capacity. What we do know is this, that there have been women of talent, and even of genius reaching near to the upper circles of the elect; and we know also that these women of marked talent have appeared whenever and wherever women have had opportunities of higher education and have been held in esteem by men as intellectual companions as well as wives and manual workers. The connection between these two facts is obvious. . . .

. . . Anyone can see that to write *Uncle Tom's Cabin* on the knee in the kitchen, with constant calls to cooking and other details of housework to punctuate the paragraphs, was a more difficult achievement than to write it at leisure in a quiet room. And when her biographer says of an Italian woman poet, "during some years her Muse was intermitted," we do not wonder at the fact when he casually mentions her ten children. No record, however, can even name the women of talent who were so submerged by childbearing and its duties, and by "general housework," that they had to leave their poems and stories all unwritten. Moreover, the obstacles to intellectual development and achievement which marriage and maternity interpose (and which are so important that they demand a separate study) are not the only ones that must be noted. It is not alone the fact that women have generally had to spend most of their strength in caring for others that has handicapped them in individual effort; but also that they have almost universally had to care wholly for themselves. Women even now have the burden of the care of their belongings, their dress, their home life of whatever sort it may be, and the social duties of the smaller world, even if doing great things in individual work. A successful woman preacher was once asked "what special obstacles have you met as a woman in the ministry?" "Not one," she answered, "except the lack of a minister's wife." When we read of Charles Darwin's wife not only relieving him from financial cares but seeing that he had his breakfast in his room, with "nothing to disturb the freshness of his morning," we do not find the explanation of Darwin's genius, but we do see how he was helped to express it. Men geniuses, even of second grade, have usually had at least one woman to smooth their way, and often several women to make sure that little things, often even self-support itself, did not interfere with the development and expression of their talent. On the other hand, the obligation of all the earlier women writers to prepare a useful cookbook in order to buy their way into literature, is a fitting symbol of the compulsion laid upon women, however gifted, to do all the things that women in general accomplish before entering upon their special task. That brave woman who wanted to study medicine so much that not even the heaviest family burdens could deter her from entering the medical school first opened to her sex, but who "first sewed steadily until her entire family was fitted with clothes to last six months," is a not unusual type.[1]

Added to all this, the woman of talent and of special gifts has had until very lately, and in most countries has still, to go against the massed social pressure of her time in order to devote herself to any particular intellectual task. The expectation of society has long pushed men toward some special work; the expectation of society has until recently been wholly against women's choosing any vocation beside their functional service in the family. This is a far more intense and all-pervading influence in deterring women from success in intellectual work than is usually understood. . . . the mildest approach on the part of a wife and mother, or even of a daughter or sister, to that intense interest in self-expression which has always characterized genius has been met with social disapproval and until very recent times with ostracism fit only for the criminal. Hence her inner impulse has needed to be strong indeed to make any woman devote herself to ideas.

1. Mrs. Thomas, graduated in first class of Women's Medical College of Philadelphia; served as City Physician at Fort Wayne, Ind., eight years.

SEVENTY YEARS AT VASSAR

On the occasion of the Vassar centennial two enterprising
editors compiled a chronicle, made up of excerpts from con-
temporary letters and other documents, that provides a fas-
cinating picture of the development of that college for women.
The excerpts here give some feel for the lives of college girls
at several different stages of the first seventy years of Vassar's
existence.

Dec. 19, 1869. The trustees refused to allow Wendell Phillips to
address Philaletheis. Indignant, Ellen Swallow wrote her mother,
"The college has been in a ferment today. . . . The committee
thought that a man so identified with radical views ought not to
come here as we were not to be exposed to radical doctrines of any
sort. . . . We are about tired of poky lectures." Caroline Hunt,
Life and Letters of Ellen H. Richards. Maria Mitchell argued "his
right to come and to say whatever he chose." Helen Wright,
Sweeper in the Sky. The trustees relented, or perhaps admitted
precedent (he had lectured at Vassar in 1867).

Feb. 24, 1870. A student wrote to her mother about the confidence she was gaining from her education: "To feel capable, not
handicapped, for the future is surely a pleasing sensation. . . ."
Letters from Old Time Vassar.

Mar. 15, 1870. "Please have my new riding basque made 22½
inches around the waist. I will have to come home in a sack if I
get much larger. . . . Dr. Avery lectured against tight lacing Tuesday morning. She never wears corsets and does not want us to."
Letters from Old Time Vassar.

Apr. 16, 1870. Describing a drawing class, one of the students
wrote: "One of the girls was putting in Raphael's darling little
cherub holding a tablet, she felt rather timid . . . and could not
make up her mind to complete the nude figure of the child. . . .
Professor [Van Ingen] exclaimed, 'What's the matter? Finish it up!

The Magnificent Enterprise: A Chronicle of Vassar College, *compiled by*
Dorothy A. Plub and George B. Dowell (Poughkeepsie: Vassar College, 1961),
pp. 18–21, 23, 27, 29, 45, 78–79. Reprinted by permission of Vassar College.

Put in everything you see. What the Lord made you don't need to be ashamed of.' It was a lesson to all of us." *Letters from Old Time Vassar.*

Apr. 29, 1870. George William Curtis, author, orator and advocate of women's rights, spoke on "Woman's Sphere is Wherever She Can Find Anything to Do." Curtis wrote a friend: "Since my lectures ended, I have written an address for the young women of Vassar College, where I went on Friday last, and to one of the most unique occasions of my whole life. The building is like the Tuileries. There are about four hundred students; and an aspect of healthfulness, intelligence and refinement, with the elegance and comfort of the college appointments, and accommodations, leaves the most delightful and cheerful impression. As you know, the spirit of the college is far from that of the 'woman's rights' movement, at least among the trustees and many of the professors, but I pleaded for perfect equality of opportunity and liberty of choice, and I was never so cordially thanked, even by those, like the president, who I thought might regret my coming.

Maria Mitchell, the astronomer, was most ardent in her expressions. Several noble-looking girls, who would not tell their names, came up to me at the reception afterwards, and asked to take my hand. I felt more than ever how deeply the best women are becoming interested." Edward Cary, *George William Curtis.*

May 10, 1870. Daily newspapers were already in use in class for the study of current history. "Must rush to the library soon to read the *World, Evening Post, Herald, Sun,* and *Tribune,* in time for our Political Economy class tomorrow or Prof. Backus will be disappointed. . . . These are some of the subjects he brings up: The Erie war carried on by the stockholders of that R.R.; transportation over the N.Y. and Erie Canal to the Gulf of Mexico; the Red River Rebellion and the Soo Canal . . . ; the Cuban difficulties . . . ; the troubles of the French and their vote taken last Sunday; the financing of their German war debt; the tariff on imported goods, etc., etc. . . . Really the large view we get of national problems interests me more than any other subject unless it is the 'woman question'. . . ." *Letters from Old Time Vassar.*

June 1, 1870. "Dr. Eliot, President of Harvard, is here. . . . He has been in at most of the recitations and told Professor Farrar that the boys at Harvard could not recite nearly as well in German, French or Latin, or even in mathematics, as the girls did here." *Letters from Old Time Vassar.*

Jan., 1871. Ellen Swallow, '70, entered Massachusetts Institute of Technology to study chemistry, the first woman to be accepted there.

May 1, 1871. The faculty minutes record that "five students have smoked cigarettes, three have drank wine, three have corresponded with Bisbee students, two of them with strangers." They were placed on probation, put on bounds, deprived of the right to have gentlemen callers, and their names and their penalties were announced in chapel "in the presence of the students."

Autumn, 1876. Harriot Stanton Blatch, '78, organized, in what she called an "institution composed entirely of a disfranchised class," a Democratic Club, the first political club at Vassar. It appealed to the disfranchised to use their *indirect* influence to elect Samuel Tilden to the presidency of the United States, and paraded through the corridors of Main, "led by a vibrant comb and jewsharp corps." *Challenging Years, Memoirs of Harriot Stanton Blatch.*

1886. The faculty adopted a new curriculum. Elizabeth H. Haight, '94, professor of Latin, 1902–42, and historian *par excellence* of Vassar College, says: "Harvard had set the example of a very free elective course. . . . Vassar's faculty . . . prepared a course of study which emphasized the need of continuity in studies, opened electives in a small degree in the latter half of the sophomore year, and made the last two years almost wholly elective." Taylor and Haight, *Vassar.* In 1895–96 the faculty allowed electives in the first semester of the sophomore year.

Sept., 1887. Lucy Maynard Salmon was appointed associate professor of history. Until this time history had been taught, in lectures, by the professor of classics and the president, although trustees and students had been discussing the introduction of a history department since 1872. A member of the class of 1874 said that she left college in advance of others of her age and sex in science, "but in history a perfect ignoramus." To raise money for Miss Salmon's salary, the students in 1886–87 voted to give up preserves once a week and to turn down the gas when they left their rooms. Her method of teaching stimulated, even shocked students and faculty accustomed to textbook authorities and memorization: she insisted on the use of original source materials, on the daily reading of the newspapers and on independent investigation by students at all levels.

Nov., 18, 1889. The faculty granted the students limited self-government. The students agreed to observe, on the honor system, the three rules regarding attendance at chapel, lights out at 10 P.M., and an hour's outdoor exercise daily.

Nov. 6, 1911. Electric lighting was installed in the Main Building. A student wrote her parents, "I am reading by the light of a gooseneck—a reading light that you can turn in almost any position. . . . We feel real scrumptious. The college gives one to each room." *MS letter.*

Nov. 27, 1911. Lady Gregory, director of the Abbey Theatre, spoke on "Making a Theatre."

Feb., 1912. The new college laundry lists included "pajamas," and the *Vassar Alumnae Monthly* commented, "The world does move."

Apr. 17, 1912. "Washington—April 17. Julia C. Lathrop, ['80] an associate of Jane Addams at Hull House, . . . a graduate and trustee of Vassar College, was appointed today by President Taft as chief of the new Children's Bureau in the Department of Commerce and Labor. Miss Lathrop is the first woman to be made chief under the government." *Poughkeepsie News-Press.*

Mar. 3, 1913. Inez Milholland, '09, led a suffrage parade in Washington. The *New York Times,* of the following day, under the headline, "1,000 Women March, Beset by Crowds," noted: "Miss Milholland was an imposing figure in a white broadcloth Cossack suit and long white kid boots. From her shoulders hung a pale blue cloak, adorned with a golden maltese cross. She was mounted on Gray Dawn, a white horse. . . ." She repeated her performance on Fifth Avenue in New York.

Apr. 13, 1913. "Our Julia Lathrop was here tonight and talked about her 'job.' Have I a birth certificate? I bet I haven't. . . . We get preached to all the time what we can do in our city gov't, especially along sanitary lines." *MS letter.*

Apr. 30, 1913. "We are having wonderful lectures in Ec now, on consumption. Professor Mills ridiculed American desire to spend, spend, spend, for the sake of spending. Vulgar shows, waste of energy and life even. He also said that women were now the leisure of the leisure classes since so much of household work has been taken away. . . . He reads copiously from Ruskin, H. G. Wells and Stevenson." *MS letter.*

May 7–12, 1934. Vassar celebrated Art Week with an exhibition of more than fifty postwar European paintings, mostly of the School of Paris, and contemporary American sculpture, including works by Picasso, Roualt, Dali, Berman, Braque, Chirico, Dufy, Ernst, Gris, Matisse, Lurçat, Tchelitchev, Lachaise, Zorach. The editors of the *Miscellany News* titled their editorial on the exhibition, "Art, Simple and Perplexed." Among the lectures this week were Jean Lurçat, William Lescaze, Edward M. Warburg and Lincoln Kirstein. The week also featured three lectures on birth control and world population.

Nov., 1934. President Roosevelt appointed Josephine Roche, '08, assistant secretary of the treasury.

Nov. 10, 1934. Gertrude Stein lectured on "Portraits I have Written and What I Think of Repetition, Whether It Exists or No," and taxied back to New York.

Feb. 19, 1935. "A bill is being proposed by a Mr. Nunan (senator) in Albany requiring every student in college . . . to take an oath to uphold the state and federal constitutions. On the surface, it is harmless enough, but actually it was suggested by Mr. Hearst to wipe out all forms of college radicalism. It would mean no pacificism or any freedom of speech or press for us. . . . Five hundred girls were at a mass meeting last night, half an hour after it was called—where Prexy and the president of students and Polit and several professors talked. Eight hundred signed a petition demanding the defeat of the bill. . . . Eighty-five of us went up [to Albany] today. . . . We disrupted the whole senate and got them to give us a general hearing this afternoon when four of our 'leaders' spoke from the floor of the senate chamber. . . ." *MS letter.*

The "march on Albany" occasioned much comment in the press and touched off controversy among alumnae. The chairman of the board of trustees said, "We are very pleased with the dignified way they conducted themselves." And an alumna pointed out, "That trip taught over ninety students what a state legislature really was." *Vassar Alumnae Magazine.*

Mar. 2, 1935. "Life is very hectic what with D.P. rehearsals, going away in the middle of the week, and John Locke's philosophy of gov't to decipher . . . he says that the Lord is the supreme judge of whether the legislative body is exceeding its authority! It is very interesting—I think my mind is beginning to sprout at last. Speaking of legislatures, the latest communication from Albany is that they are favorable to the passage of the Nunan bill. Have you seen any of the Hearst editorials? esp. the one saying that the Vassar girls ought to be sent to bed on bread and water?" *MS letter.* The Nunan bill was defeated.

Apr., 1935. Vassar students joined the picket line at the Werber Leather Coat Company at Beacon, N.Y. A student wrote home: "Monday afternoon we took the train for Beacon—we talked to the strikers and employees . . . then, since the strikers were very, oh so very, obviously in the right, since the managers were violating every hour and wage rule of the NRA, we joined in the picketing. . . . Here, the public opinion is pretty stiff, and we're not feeling too comfortable, but the faculty are nice to me, and my friends all understand. . . . By the way, it wasn't a radical group of girls that went down, most of them were very respectable. I'm not trying to offer any excuses, I did what I thought was right, and was very glad I had done it—we did save the strike for them, there *is* a place where we can help. . . ." *MS letter.*

WHERE ARE WE NOW?

We must presume that Mrs. Mott's heart would be rejoiced if she could witness the present educational opportunities for women. Have these, indeed, led to the "elevation" she spoke of? The subject could occupy a whole book by itself. In this selection two Columbia University sociologists indulge in some reflections about the forces that shape the lives of highly educated women in this society.

Eli Ginzberg and Alice M. Yohalem, Educated American Women: Self-Portraits (New York: Columbia University Press, 1966), pp. 3–8. Reprinted by permission of the publisher.

The lives that women and, for that matter, men, lead reflect two sets of major forces. The first is composed of the external environment with its complex of opportunities and constraints. The second reflects the values and goals of the individual who, always with some margins for discretion, must determine what he most wants and the price he is willing to pay for it.

The extent of transformation which takes place in the role of women is an important index of the rate of social change. The more rigid the society, the more fixed is the pattern of life which women must follow. In the United States, major changes have occurred in the structure and functioning of society during the present century, and these have led to fundamental transformations in the patterning of women's lives.

Changes in the lives of educated women in the post–World War II decades can be appreciated only against a background of the more important changes that took place during the preceding generations in the world of work on the one hand and in the home on the other.

By the turn of this century the United States was well on the way to becoming an industrialized urban society. The majority of the population lived in urban centers. The factory system was well established. The tertiary stage of economic development—the expansion of the service sector—was proceeding rapidly while the number engaged in agriculture was nearing its peak and manufacturing was still experiencing a rapid growth. . . .

However, these broad changes in the environment at large merely set the limits within which plans and adaptations are carried out. A second set of forces, individual values and goals, is of equal importance in influencing a woman's style of life. The specific life patterns that a woman develops depend on three strategic variables: the shaping of her personality, the immediate circumstances of her adult life, and the way in which she responds to these circumstances.

Although a woman's genetic endowment is, of course, crucial to the character of her personality, the environment in which she grows up determines in considerable measure the type of goals and values she develops. The most significant influence is the family into which she is born and reared. Her parents play a large role in the determination of the amount and type of education she acquires and this, in turn, affects her interests and outlook. Her parents' values influence her definition of her future role. They can encourage the development of a goal which stresses a career or marriage, or a balance between a career and marriage. They can provide a home that stimulates the development of ideas, interests, and capacities or one that furnishes limited opportunities for self-realization. . . .

No matter what plan a young woman develops for her life and work, her ability to realize her goals will be influenced by the circumstances of her adult life. If she remains single, she usually has no choice but to support herself by engaging in full-time work. If she marries while she is in school, her husband's income may help to determine the extent of her education, since she may have to interrupt her own studies to help him to complete his. After she has her children, her husband's earnings will largely determine whether she can afford household help which in turn will affect her ability to hold a job.

Her husband's career may impose limitations on her own work. If he is transferred frequently, it may be difficult even for a well-prepared woman to pursue her career systematically because of limited opportunities in many communities. A woman often marries a man in the same or an allied field and she may find that many institutions, especially colleges and universities, will not hire more than one member of a family.

The husband himself can also exercise a determining influence on the patterning of his wife's work and life. If he holds a negative attitude about a woman's working, he may interpose so many objections that his wife will forego a career in order to save the marriage. Another husband may take a diametrically opposite stance; he may push his wife into further education and work even though she prefers to remain at home with her children.

Another significant set of circumstances results from the presence of children. Depending on the number and, particularly, the ages of her children, a woman is under more or less pressure to adjust the pattern of her life to their needs and demands. While, as we have noted, a woman can regulate the number and spacing of her children, she cannot always predict the constraints and pressures that a growing family may exert on her plans for a career.

We see, then, that her husband's income, his job, his attitudes, and the needs of her children all go far to determine the character of a woman's activities. In addition, there are restrictions due to the fact that many employers are reluctant to hire women.

The third determining factor is the response that a woman makes to the particular circumstances she encounters. There are many different ways in which women can cope with the same objective circumstances. For instance, one woman may decide to work only if taking a job will yield the family a net increment in income. Another may decide to work as long as taking a job costs her nothing. In a family with some margins, a woman may work even if her salary does not cover the expenses incurred by her employment.

Some women are willing to leave their children to the care of a maid; others will work only if a close relative cares for the children; still others insist upon bringing up their children themselves.

Some women who want to combine home and work will put forth a great amount of physical and emotional effort in order to meet their responsibilities in each sphere. Others will not or cannot expend so much energy and time; they either cut down their obligations at work or cut corners in their homemaking or make adjustments in both. Some mothers wish to spend their free time in paid employment; others choose to utilize their skills and pursue their interests by engaging in volunteer work or in creative leisure activities; still others think of homemaking and childrearing as full-time activities.

These are some of the many different ways in which women respond to given sets of circumstances. Their responses are determined by a type of balance sheet of sacrifices and rewards. This reflects, first, the importance each woman attaches to realizing specific values and accomplishing specific goals in the various areas of her life. In addition, the entries reflect the costs which she ascribes to different actions which she must take to realize her values and goals.

Before the turn of the century alternative patterns of life were determined to a great extent by a more or less rigid environment. A woman who had completed higher education could generally pursue a career only at the cost of foregoing marriage and a family. If she married she had to withdraw from work and devote her abilities and energies to raising her children and participating in voluntary activities. Her alternatives were a career *or* marriage.

Because of the revolutionary changes which have taken place in the environment, these limited alternatives have been significantly broadened. A woman is now able to work while she is studying, before her marriage, after she marries, while her children are very young, after they enter school, or after they have grown up. Or she may decide not to work. Moreover, even if she decides to follow one pattern, she can shift to another. For example, if she finds that her decision to work while her children are very young is unsatisfactory she may resign from her job. Or the reverse may happen. She may stop working at the birth of her first child anticipating that she will remain out of the labor market until her youngest child enters grade school, only to find that she cannot tolerate a life of total domesticity.

Chapter 4

Reform

There has been an important relationship between reform movements and the emergence of American women into a public role. As some women tried to change the world, they changed themselves. Early in the nineteenth century, women active in the abolition movement were also among the first to speak out about women's rights. Since men often talked about the superior moral sensitivity of women, there was a certain logic to the tendency of women to become interested in the human problems of an industrial civilization. At the same time, women reformers developed confidence and competence and became models for aspiring younger women.

THE EFFECT OF REFORM ACTIVITY
ON WOMEN'S PERSONALITIES

One of the most interesting aspects of the tendency of women to take part in reform movements was the effect such activity had upon a woman's personality. Antifeminists had their own theories about this: that unladylike activity turned women into unattractive monsters. In this selection Ida Husted Harper reflects upon the effect her work in the suffrage movement had upon Susan B. Anthony.

Considerable space has been given to detailed accounts of these early [Women's Rights] conventions to illustrate the prejudice

Ida Husted Harper, The Life and Work of Susan B. Anthony (*Indianapolis and Kansas City, Bobbs Merrill, 1899*), vol. 1, pp. 107–8.

which existed against woman's speaking in public, and the martyrdom suffered by the pioneers to secure the right of free speech for
succeeding generations. From this time until the merging of all
questions into the Civil War, such conventions were held every
year, producing a great revolution of sentiment in the direction
of an enlarged sphere for woman's activities and a modification of
the legal and religious restraints that so long had held her in
bondage. They have been fully described also in order to indicate
some of the causes which operated in the development of the mind
and character of Susan B. Anthony, transforming her by degrees
from a quiet, domestic Quaker maiden to a strong, courageous,
uncompromising advocate of absolute equality of rights for woman.
Brought into close association with the most advanced men and
women of the age, seeing on every hand the injustice perpetrated
against her sex and hearing the magnificent appeals for the liberty
of every human being, her soul could not fail to respond; and
having passed the age when women are apt to consecrate themselves to love and marriage, it was most natural that she should
dedicate her services to the struggle for the freedom of woman.
She did not realize then that this would reach through fifty years
of exacting and unending toil, but even had she done so, who can
doubt that she freely would have given up her life to the work?

In the ten weeks before the state convention at Albany, 6,000
names were secured for the petition that married women should
be entitled to the wages they earned and to the equal guardianship of their children, and 4,000 asking for the suffrage. Miss Anthony herself trudged from house to house during that stormy
winter, many of the women slamming the door in her face with
the statement that they "had all the rights they wanted"; although
at this time an employer was bound by law to pay the wife's wages
to the husband, and the father had the power to apprentice young
children without the mother's consent, and even to dispose of them
by will at his death. One minister, in Rochester, after looking her
over carefully, said: "Miss Anthony, you are too fine a physical
specimen of woman to be doing such work as this. You ought to
marry and have children." Ignoring the insult, she replied in a
dignified manner: "I think it a much wiser thing to secure for the
thousands of mothers in this state the legal control of the children
they now have, than to bring others into the world who would not
belong to me after they were born."

The state convention met in Association Hall, Albany, February 14, 1854. Elizabeth Cady Stanton, president, delivered a magnificent address which Miss Anthony had printed and laid upon the desk of every member of the legislature; she also circulated 50,000 of these pamphlets throughout the state. The convention had been called for two days, but so great was the interest aroused and so popular were the speakers in attendance that evening meetings were held for two weeks; the questions under consideration were taken up by the newspapers of Albany and the discussion spread through the press of the state, finding able defenders as well as bitter opponents.

THE DEMAND FOR THE VOTE

Women worked hard for abolition, and when the Civil War ended in victory for the North they assumed that they, along with the newly freed slaves, would receive the right to vote. Male abolitionists were of another opinion: the women should wait in order not to jeopardize the chances of the Negroes. Elizabeth Cady Stanton tried to explain why women needed the vote as badly as the blacks did.

"Individual rights," "individual conscience and judgment," are great American ideas, underlying our whole political and religious life. We are here today to ask a Congress of Republicans for that crowning act that shall secure to 15,000,000 women the right to protect their persons, property, and opinions by law. The Fourteenth Amendment, having told us who are citizens of the republic, further declares that "no State shall make or enforce any law which shall abridge the 'privileges or immunities' of 'citizens' of the United States." Some say that "privileges and immunities" do not include the right of suffrage. We answer that any person under government who has no voice in the laws or the rulers has his privileges and immunities abridged at every turn, and when a state denies the right of suffrage, it robs the citizen of his citizenship and of all power to protect his person or property by law.

Disfranchised classes are ever helpless and degraded classes. One

E. C. Stanton, Susan B. Anthony and M. J. Gage, History of Woman Suffrage (Rochester: Susan B. Anthony, 1887), vol. 2, pp. 508–10.

can readily judge of the political status of a citizen by the tone of the press. Go back a few years, and you find the Irishman the target for all the gibes and jeers of the nation. You could scarce take up a paper without finding some joke about "Pat" and his last bull. But in process of time "Pat" became a political power in the land, and editors and politicians could not afford to make fun of him. Then "Sambo" took his turn. They ridiculed his thick skull, woolly head, shinbone, long heel, etc., but he, too, has become a political power; he sits in the Congress of the United States and in the legislature of Massachusetts, and now politicians and editors can not afford to make fun of him.

Now, who is their target? Woman. They ridicule all alike—the strong-minded for their principles, the weak-minded for their panniers. How long think you the New York *Tribune* would maintain its present scurrilous tone if the votes of women could make Horace Greeley governor of New York? The editor of the *Tribune* knows the value of votes, and if, honorable gentlemen, you will give us a "declaratory law," forbidding the states to deny or abridge our rights, there will be no need of arguments to change the tone of his journal; its columns will speedily glow with demands for the protection of woman as well as broadcloth and pig iron. Then we might find out what he knows and cares for our real and relative value in the government.

Without some act of Congress regulating suffrage for women as well as black men, women citizens of the United States who, in Washington, Utah, and Wyoming Territories, are voters and jurors, and who, in the state of Kansas, vote on school and license questions, would be denied the exercise of their right to vote in all the states of the Union, and no naturalization papers, education, property, residence, or age could help them. What an anomaly is this in a republic! A woman who in Wyoming enjoys all the rights, privileges, and immunities of a sovereign, by crossing the line into Nebraska, sinks at once to the political degradation of a slave. Humiliated with such injustice, one set of statesmen answer her appeals by sending her for redress to the courts; another advises her to submit her qualifications to the states; but we, with a clearer intuition of the rightful power, come to you who thoughtfully, conscientiously, and understandingly passed that amendment defining the word "citizen," declaring suffrage a foundation right. How are women "citizens" from Utah, Wyoming, Kansas, moving in other states, to be protected in the rights they have heretofore enjoyed, unless Congress shall pass the bill presented by Mr. Butler, and thus give us a homogeneous law on suffrage from Maine to Louisiana? Remember, these are citizens of the United States as well as of the territories and states wherein they may reside, and their rights as such are of primal consideration. One of your own amendments to the federal Constitution, honorable gentlemen, says "that the right of citizens of the United States to vote shall not be denied or abridged by any State on account of race, color, or previous condition of servitude." We have women of different races and colors, as well as men. It takes more than men to compose peoples and races, and no one denies that all women suffer the disabilities of a present or previous condition of servitude. Clearly the state may regulate, but can not deny the exercise of this right to any citizen.

You did not leave the Negroes to the tender mercies of the courts and states. Why send your mothers, wives, and daughters suppliants at the feet of the unwashed, unlettered, unthinking masses that carry our elections in the states? Would you compel the women of New York to sue the Tweeds, the Sweeneys, the Connollys, for their inalienable rights, or to have the scales of justice balanced for them in the unsteady hand of a Cardozo, a Barnard, or a McCunn? Nay, nay; the proper tribunal to decide nice questions of human rights and constitutional interpretations, the political status of every citizen under our national flag, is the Congress of the United States. This is your right and duty, clearly set forth in article 1, section 5, of the Constitution, for how can you decide the competency and qualifications of electors for members of either house without settling the fundamental question on what the right of suffrage is based? All power centers in the people. Our federal Constitution, as well as that of every state, opens with the words, "We, the people." However this phrase may have been understood and acted on in the past, women today are awake to the fact that they constitute one-half the American people; that they have the right to demand that the Constitution shall secure to them "justice," "domestic tranquillity," and the "blessings of liberty." So long as women are not represented in the government they are in a condition of tutelage, perpetual minority, slavery.

You smile at the idea of women being slaves in this country. Benjamin Franklin said long ago, "that they who have no voice in making the laws, or in the election of those who administer them, do not enjoy liberty, but are absolutely enslaved to those who have votes and to their representatives." I might occupy hours in quoting grand liberal sentiments from the fathers—Madison, Jefferson, Otis, and Adams—in favor of individual representation. I might quote equally noble words from the statesmen of our day—Seward, Sumner, Wade, Trumbull, Schurz, Thurman, Groesbeck, and Julian—to prove "that no just government can be formed without the consent of the governed"; that "the ballot is the columbiad of our political life, and every man who holds it is a full-armed monitor." But what do lofty utterances and logical arguments avail so long as men, blinded by old prejudices and customs, fail to see their application to the women by their side? Alas! gentlemen, women are your subjects. Your own selfish interests are too closely interwoven for you to feel their degradation, and they are too dependent to reveal themselves to you in their nobler aspirations, their native dignity. Did Southern slaveholders ever understand the humiliations of slavery to a proud man like Frederick Douglass? Did the coarse, low-bred master ever doubt his capacity to govern the Negro better than he could govern himself? Do cowboys, hostlers, pot-house politicians ever doubt their capacity to prescribe woman's sphere better than she could herself? We have yet to learn that, with the wonderful progress in art, science, education, morals, religion, and government we have witnessed in the last century, woman has not been standing still, but has been gradually advancing to an equal place with the man by her side, and stands today his peer in the world of thought.

American womanhood has never worn iron shoes, burned on the funeral pile, or skulked behind a mask in a harem, yet, though cradled in liberty, with the same keen sense of justice and equality that man has, she is still bound by law in the swaddling bands of an old barbarism. Though the world has been steadily advancing in political science, and step by step recognizing the rights of new classes, yet we stand today talking of precedents, authorities, laws, and constitutions, as if each generation were not better able to judge of its wants than the one that preceded it. If we are to be governed in all things by the men of the eighteenth century, and the twentieth by the nineteenth, and so on, the world will be always governed by dead men. The exercise of political power by woman is by no means a new idea. It has already been exercised in many countries, and under governments far less liberal in theory than our own. As to this being an innovation on the laws of nature, we may safely trust nature at all times to vindicate herself. In England, where the right to vote is based on property and not person, the *feme sole* freeholder has exercised her right all along. In her earliest history we find records of decisions in courts of her right to do so, and discussions on that point by able lawyers and judges. The *feme sole* voted in person; when married, her husband represented her property, and voted in her stead; and the moment the breath went out of his body, she assumed again the burden of disposing of her own income and the onerous duty of representing herself in the government. Thus England is always consistent; property being the basis of suffrage, is always represented. Here suffrage is based on "persons," and yet one-half our people are wholly unrepresented.

We have declared in favor of a government of the people, for the people, by the people, the whole people. Why not begin the experiment? If suffrage is a natural right, we claim it in common with all citizens. . . .

HARD WORK IN THEIR OWN BEHALF

Angry at having been omitted from the Fourteenth Amendment, suffrage leaders kept on working both in state campaigns and in presenting, over and over, a proposed constitutional amendment to the Congress. Anna Howard Shaw described one of her numerous campaign trips in the West.

That South Dakota campaign was one of the most difficult we ever made. It extended over nine months; and it is impossible to describe the poverty which prevailed throughout the whole rural community of the state. There had been three consecutive years of drought. The sand was like powder, so deep that the wheels of the wagons in which we rode "across country" sank halfway to the hubs; and in the midst of this dry powder lay withered tangles that had once been grass. Everyone had the forsaken, desperate

Anna Howard Shaw, The Story of a Pioneer (New York: Harper & Brothers, 1915), pp. 200–4. Copyright 1915 by Harper & Brothers; renewed 1943 by Lucy E. Anthony. Reprinted by permission of Harper & Row, Publishers, Inc.

look worn by the pioneer who has reached the limit of his endurance, and the great stretches of prairie roads showed innumerable canvas-covered wagons, drawn by starved horses, and followed by starved cows, on their way "Back East." Our talks with the despairing drivers of these wagons are among my most tragic memories. They had lost everything except what they had with them, and they were going East to leave "the woman" with her father and try to find work. Usually, with a look of disgust at his wife, the man would say: "I wanted to leave two years ago, but the woman kept saying, 'Hold on a little longer.'"

Both Miss Anthony and I gloried in the spirit of these pioneer women, and lost no opportunity to tell them so; for we realized what our nation owes to the patience and courage of such as they were. We often asked them what was the hardest thing to bear in their pioneer life, and we usually received the same reply:

"To sit in our little adobe or sod houses at night and listen to the wolves howl over the graves of our babies. For the howl of the wolf is like the cry of a child from the grave."

Many days, and in all kinds of weather, we rode forty and fifty miles in uncovered wagons. Many nights we shared a one-room cabin with all the members of the family. But the greatest hardship we suffered was the lack of water. There was very little good water in the state, and the purest water was so brackish that we could hardly drink it. The more we drank the thirstier we became, and when the water was made into tea it tasted worse than when it was clear. A bath was the rarest of luxuries. The only available fuel was buffalo manure, of which the odor permeated all our food. But despite these handicaps we were happy in our work, for we had some great meetings and many wonderful experiences.

When we reached the Black Hills we had more of this genuine campaigning. We traveled over the mountains in wagons, behind teams of horses, visiting the mining camps; and often the gullies were so deep that when our horses got into them it was almost impossible to get them out. I recall with special clearness one ride from Hill City to Custer City. It was only a matter of thirty miles, but it was thoroughly exhausting; and after our meeting that same night we had to drive forty miles farther over the mountains to get the early morning train from Buffalo Gap. The trail from Custer City to Buffalo Gap was the one the animals had originally made in their journeys over the pass, and the drive in that wild region, throughout a cold, piercing October night, was an unforgetable experience. Our host at Custer City lent Miss Anthony his big buffalo overcoat, and his wife lent hers to me. They also heated blocks of wood for our feet, and with these protections we started. A full moon hung in the sky. The trees were covered with hoar-frost, and the cold, still air seemed to sparkle in the brilliant light. Again Miss Anthony talked to me throughout the night—of the work, always of the work, and of what it would mean to the women who followed us; and again she fired my soul with the flame that burned so steadily in her own.

It was daylight when we reached the little station at Buffalo Gap where we were to take the train. This was not due, however, for half an hour, and even then it did not come. The station was only large enough to hold the stove, the ticket office, and the inevitable cuspidor. There was barely room in which to walk be-tween these and the wall. Miss Anthony sat down on the floor. I had a few raisins in my bag, and we divided them for breakfast. An hour passed, and another, and still the train did not come. Miss Anthony, her back braced against the wall, buried her face in her hands and dropped into a peaceful abyss of slumber, while I walked restlessly up and down the platform. The train arrived four hours late, and when eventually we had reached our desti-nation we learned that the ministers of the town had persuaded the women to give up the suffrage meeting scheduled for that night, as it was Sunday.

This disappointment, following our all-day and all-night drive to keep our appointment, aroused Miss Anthony's fighting spirit. She sent me out to rent the theater for the evening, and to have some handbills printed and distributed, announcing that we would speak. At three o'clock she made the concession to her seventy years of lying down for an hour's rest. I was young and vigorous, so I trotted around town to get somebody to preside, somebody to intro-duce us, somebody to take up the collection, and somebody who would provide music—in short, to make all our preparations for the night meeting.

When evening came the crowd which had assembled was so great that men and women sat in the windows and on the stage, and stood in the flies. Night attractions were rare in that Dakota town, and here was something new. Nobody went to church, so the churches were forced to close. We had a glorious meeting. Both

Miss Anthony and I were in excellent fighting trim, and Miss Anthony remarked that the only thing lacking to make me do my best was a sick headache. The collection we took up paid all our expenses, the church singers sang for us, the great audience was interested, and the whole occasion was an inspiring success.

The meeting ended about half after ten o'clock, and I remember taking Miss Anthony to our hotel and escorting her to her room. I also remember that she followed me to the door and made some laughing remark as I left for my own room; but I recall nothing more until the next morning when she stood beside me telling me it was time for breakfast. She had found me lying on the cover of my bed, fully clothed even to my bonnet and shoes. I had fallen there, utterly exhausted, when I entered my room the night before; and I do not think I had even moved from that time until the moment—nine hours later—when I heard her voice and felt her hand on my shoulder.

After all our work, we did not win Dakota that year, but Miss Anthony bore the disappointment with the serenity she always showed. To her a failure was merely another opportunity, and I mention our experience here only to show of what she was capable in her gallant seventies. *— fantastic —*

OPPOSITION

Not least of the reasons that working for their own suffrage was a "growing experience" for women was the depth of feeling expressed by the opposition. Many people, men and women, were frightened by the prospect of changes in women's life patterns. Many of the opposition arguments appeared in an article in The Independent in 1901.

. . . But it is now obvious to impartial observers that these "rights" are in reality demanded by only a very small group of women—mostly mannish women, too, belonging to what has been aptly called "the third sex"; and that to grant them the "rights" demanded would in reality be to inflict a grievous *wrong* on the vast majority of women—the womanly women—as well as on chil-

Henry T. Finck, *"Are Womanly Women Doomed,"* The Independent *53* (January 1901): 269–70.

dren, on men, and on society in general. Here lies the gist of the whole matter.

A favorite question of the few women who want the suffrage is, "Why not let those of us vote who want to?" This very question shows their unfitness for the franchise. It puts them on a level with naughty children who want to do certain things regardless of consequences to themselves and others. All students of our political life know that its greatest danger lies in the difficulty of getting the better class of men to vote and attend to their civic duties, whereas the rabble, headed by demagogs and rascals, always votes. With refined women the difficulty of getting them to vote would be greater still. The rabble, which in both sexes has a majority, would therefore be doubled, while the educated—*including the woman suffragists themselves*—would be left in a helpless minority; wherefore it is the duty of legislators to protect these women against their own folly by refusing them the ballot.

If the danger of doubling the power of the ignorant and the vicious were not alone sufficient to condemn equal suffrage, there is another consideration which would give it the *coup de grâce*. With all their "blatant assumptions" and "wild vagaries" none of the female suffragists have ever gone quite so far as to demand that men should play *second* fiddle in politics. Yet this is what would inevitably happen if women were allowed to vote and took advantage of their privilege. For in most civilized countries there are more women than men, wherefore the men would be outvoted and the women might assume all the offices, from the presidency down. Then, truly, might the poet sing, "all the world's a stage"— and the play a topsy-turvy Gilbert and Sullivan operetta. Legislators are not likely to go into this burlesque business in a hurry.

Not only would woman's participation in political life take away man's supremacy in a field in which he has always, as a matter of course, played the leading part (except among a few barbarous tribes whose women were as masculine as the men), but it would involve the domestic calamity of a deserted home and the loss of the womanly qualities for which refined men adore women and marry them. "Motherhood," in the words of Bishop Doane, would be "replaced by mannishness," and "neglected homes" would "furnish candidates for mismanaged offices." To children the political activity demanded as a "right" would be a still greater wrong in often depriving them of a mother's care when most needed. Doctors tell us, too, that thousands of children would be harmed or killed before birth by the injurious effect of untimely political excitement on their mothers.

All these crimes, calamities and absurdities legislators are asked to countenance simply to please a handful of discontented women who clamor for "rights" which they have never been able to prove that they need in the least. Women were once the absolute slaves of men. Without any right to vote they have been gradually emancipated, until now, as Professor Goldwin Smith has remarked, "the attitude of men in the United States toward women is rather that of subjection than that of domination"; and in some states the pendulum has really swung too far. These concessions were made from a sense of gallantry and justice. Were women allowed to vote sex antagonism would be substituted for gallantry. "The arrogant assertion of demanded rights" would, to cite once more the happy phraseology of Bishop Doane, destroy "the instinctive chivalry of conceded courtesies." Of all the mistakes made by the equal suffragists, none is more ridiculous than their naive assumption that when women shall have become angry opponents in place of gentle companions and helpers, men will retain their chivalrous deference to them and refrain from using their brute force in an emergency.

If the suffragists alone were to be the sufferers one might teach them a lesson by giving them a trial of what they want; but it would be a great wrong to the womanly women to expose them to a loss of men's gallantry and at the same time to all the nastiness and villainy of political strife. It is indeed assumed that women would refine political life by imparting to it their gentleness, tenderness and delicacy; but as Goldwin Smith pertinently asks:

> Is it not because they have been kept out of politics and generally out of the contentious arena that they have remained gentle, tender, and delicate?

Politics in Colorado is, as Pastor Ryan testifies, "the same old dirty game" it was before women took part in it; and no worldly wise person endowed with an imagination can doubt that it would habitually degrade women instead of elevating men. It is infinitely easier to break a fine vase than to make one.

OPPOSITION FROM A WOMAN

The "antis" who opposed the women's rights movement were not all male. Here a woman chastises her sisters for their discontent.

. . . There has never been a time in the world's history, when female discontent has assumed so much, and demanded so much, as at the present day; and both the satisfied and the dissatisfied woman may well pause to consider, whether the fierce fever of unrest which has possessed so large a number of the sex is not rather a <u>delirium</u> than a conviction; whether indeed they are not just as foolishly impatient to get out of their Eden, as was the woman Eve six thousand years ago.

We may premise, in order to clear the way, that there is a noble discontent which has a great work to do in the world; a discontent which is the antidote to conceit and self-satisfaction, and which urges the worker of every kind continually to realize a higher ideal. . . .

Having acknowledged so much in favor of discontent, we may now consider some of the most objectionable forms in which it has attacked certain women of our own generation. In the van of these malcontents are the women dissatisfied with their home duties. One of the saddest domestic features of the day is the disrepute into which <u>housekeeping</u> has fallen; for that is <u>a woman's first natural duty and answers to the needs of her best nature</u>. It is by no means necessary that she should be a Cinderella among the ashes, . . . or a Penelope for ever at her needle, but all women of intelligence now understand that good cooking is a liberal science, and that there is a most intimate connection between food and virtue, and food and health, and food and thought. Indeed, many things are called crimes that are not as bad as the savagery of an Irish cook or the messes of a fourth-rate confectioner.

It must be noted that this revolt of certain women against housekeeping is not a revolt against their husbands; it is simply a revolt

Mrs. Amelia Barr, "Discontented Women," North American Review 162 (1896): 202–3.

against their duties. They consider house-work hard and monotonous and inferior, and confess with a cynical frankness that they
prefer to engross paper, or dabble in art, or embroider pillow-
shams, or sell goods, or in some way make money to pay servants
who will cook their husband's dinner and nurse their babies for
them. And they believe that in this way they show themselves to
have superior minds, and ask credit for a deed which ought to
cover them with shame. For actions speak louder than words, and
what does such action say? In the first place, it asserts that any
stranger—even a young uneducated peasant girl hired for a few
dollars a month—is able to perform the duties of the house-mistress
and the mother. In the second place, it substitutes a poor ambition
for love, and hand service for heart service. In the third place, it is
a visible abasement of the loftiest duties of womanhood to the
capacity of the lowest paid service. A wife and mother can not thus
absolve her own soul; she simply disgraces and traduces her holiest
work. . . .

Fortunately, the vast majority of women have been loyal to their
sex and their vocation. In every community the makers and keepers
of homes are the dominant power; and these strictures can apply
only to two classes—first, the married women who neglect husband,
children and homes, for the foolish *eclát* of the club and the platform, or for any assumed obligation, social, intellectual or political,
which conflicts with their domestic duties: secondly, the unmarried
women who, having comfortable homes and loving protectors, are
discontent with their happy secluded security and rush into weak
art or feeble literature, or dubious singing and acting, because their
vanity and restless immorality lead them into the market place, or
on to the stage. Not one of such women has been driven afield by
indisputable genius. Any work they have done would have been
better done by some unprotected experienced woman already in
the fields they have invaded. And the indifference of this class to
the money value of their labor has made it difficult for the women
working because they must work or starve, to get a fair price for
their work. It is the baldest effrontery for this class of rich discon-
tents to affect sympathy with Woman's Progress. Nothing can excuse their intrusion into the labor market but unquestioned genius
and super-excellence of work; and this has not yet been shown in
any single case.

SURVEYING THE ACCOMPLISHMENT
OF SUFFRAGE

It was 1920 before all American women were finally able to vote. Carrie Chapman Catt, who organized the final drive that helped to win Congress and the state legislatures to woman suffrage, reflected on the magnitude of the effort.

When, during the last decade, the great suffrage parades—armies of women with banners, orange and black, yellow and blue and purple and green and gold—went marching through the streets of the cities and towns of America; when "suffrage canvassers," knocking at the doors of America, were a daily sight; when the suffragist on the soapbox was heard on every street corner; when huge suffrage mass meetings were packing auditoriums from end to end of the country; when lively "suffrage stunts" were rousing and stirring the public; when suffrage was in everybody's mouth and on the front page of every newspaper, few paused to ask how it all started, where it all came from. It was just there, like breakfast.

To the unimaginative man on the street corner, watching one of those suffrage parades, the long lines of marching women may have seemed to come out of nowhere, to have no starting place, no connection with his grandmother and his great-grandmother. To the same man the insistent tapping of those suffrage canvassers, the commotion of the suffrage mass meetings, the repetition of those suffrage stunts, the incessant news of suffrage in the daily press, may have seemed unrelated acts irrelevant to social history. Yet it was all part of social history, and had immediate connection with other phases of social history. For the demand for woman suffrage was the logical outcome of two preceding social movements, both extending over some centuries: one, a man movement, evolving toward control of governments by the people, the other a woman movement, with its goal the freeing of women from the masculine tutelage to which law, religion, tradition and custom bound them.

Carrie Chapman Catt and Nettie Rogers Shuler, Woman Suffrage and Politics *(New York: Charles Scribner's Sons, 1926), pp. 3–4, 266–67. Reprinted by permission of the publisher.*

These movements advanced in parallel lines and the enfranchisement of woman was an inevitable climax of both. . . .

In the suffrage army more than two millions of women were enlisted. The parent body, the National American Woman Suffrage Association, directed the activities of the great mass of them, while the Woman's Party projected its entirely separate and often conflicting program for the group of militants. When victory finally perched upon the banners of the suffragists the National Suffrage Association had direct auxiliaries in forty-six states of the Union and these far-reaching confederated bodies were functioning as one organ through its centralized national board. Extensive headquarters were maintained in both Washington and New York. In Washington congressional activities radiated from the great house at 1626 Rhode Island Avenue. In New York headquarters occupied two entire floors, equivalent to thirty large rooms, of a business building, 171 Madison Avenue. Between forty and fifty women were continuously retained on the clerical staff, and as many field workers were engaged in campaigns. A publishing company prepared and printed literature of various kinds. Publicity, organization, data and educational departments constituted branches of the general administration, and a weekly thirty-two-page magazine, the *Woman Citizen,* was maintained as the association's official organ and mouthpiece.

Historically, the National American Woman Suffrage Association presents a record of intensive organization probably never paralleled. Through half a century of incessant work that record reaches back to 1869. Even fifteen years before that time suffrage work of an agitational kind had been conducted by local committees or clubs under the direction of a strongly centralized national board. That plan of organization served the purposes of the early time admirably, but when it became clear that the women must for a time go to the states to seek and win the suffrage by referenda campaigns, a different form of organization was found necessary. The workers, therefore, by common consent in 1869, prepared the way for a new body better adapted to the new phase of the struggle. Out of the process, two organizations emerged—The National Woman Suffrage Association and The American Woman Suffrage Association, the first led by Elizabeth Cady Stanton and Susan B. Anthony, the second by Lucy Stone, the differences being more personal than tactical.

The aims of both were the same, to secure suffrage for women whenever possible and by any constitutional method. The National emphasized the federal suffrage method by holding annual conventions in Washington and securing hearings on the Federal Suffrage Amendment, but it maintained, too, the policy of winning woman suffrage state by state until enough states should have adopted it to make woman voters an element no longer negligible in the constituencies of United States congressmen who would some day vote on the Federal Suffrage Amendment. The "American" concentrated on state campaigns with the same end in view, whenever federal action should be possible. The field was wide and by tacit consent the two organizations kept out of each other's way, only a few states having auxiliaries to both.

Twenty years later the younger recruits, perceiving that the two separate organizations at times conflicted, set themselves to the task of union. This they successfully accomplished in 1890, the National-American Woman Suffrage Association resulting, with this announced aim:

> The object of this association shall be to secure protection in their right to vote to the women citizens of the United States by appropriate national and state legislation.

Auxiliary to this national body were the state suffrage organizations, known by various titles. They paid dues and sent delegates to the annual conventions where officers were elected, reports heard and plans made. The annual conventions were dated from 1869, although they had been held continuously since 1850, except during the war period.

WHAT IT TOOK

Mrs. Catt spoke in another place of what it took to get the vote for women in the United States.

To get that word, male, out of the Constitution, cost the women of this country 52 years of pauseless campaign; 56 state referendum campaigns; 480 legislative campaigns to get state suffrage amend-

Mary Gray Peck, Carrie Chapman Catt, A Biography (*New York: The H. W. Wilson Company, 1944*), *pp. 5–6. Reprinted by permission of the publisher.*

ments submitted; 47 state constitutional convention campaigns; 277 state party convention campaigns; 30 national party convention campaigns to get suffrage planks in the party platforms; 19 campaigns with 19 successive Congresses to get the federal amendment submitted, and the final ratification campaign.

Millions of dollars were raised, mostly in small sums, and spent with economic care. Hundreds of women gave the accumulated possibilities of an entire lifetime, thousands gave years of their lives, hundreds of thousands gave constant interest and such aid as they could. It was a continuous and seemingly endless chain of activity. Young suffragists who helped forge the last links of that chain were not born when it began. Old suffragists who helped forge the first links were dead when it ended.

CLUBS AS INSTRUMENTS OF REFORM

All over the United States in the 1870s and '80s women began to form themselves into clubs for "culture," sociability, and—as it turned out—social reform. The initial impulse was often a need for intellectual stimulation, but in time many women decided the world, or at least their local communities, needed them. A woman reporter who had helped with the effort to limit child labor described the work of club women.

About this time also I allied myself with the federated women's clubs. I had been reporting club activities for several years without any impulse to become a club member. I respected the movement as a whole, but in those early days its adherents were occupied almost entirely with a form of culture which I already possessed. The women studied Dante, Browning, the drama, art, opera, and the musical glasses, reading papers to their fellows at elaborate luncheons and tea-parties. They were beginning to take up education, child labor and village improvement as side lines, but serious questions, especially woman suffrage, were taboo. However, at the national Biennial Convention held in St. Louis in 1904, the whole club movement took a tremendous spurt forward. Not only did the program include a discussion, pro and con, of suffrage, but a woman

Rheta Childe Dorr, A Woman of Fifty *(New York: Funk & Wagnalls Company, 1924), pp. 118–20. Reprinted by permission of the publisher.*

voter was elected president of the General Federation. This was Sarah Platt Decker of Denver, a truly great woman, highly educated, widely traveled, experienced in politics, a woman whose sex alone kept her from being a United States Senator from Colorado.

Mrs. Decker did not seek the presidency of the federation, but after her informative and forceful speech in the suffrage discussion, the office was literally forced upon her. . . . Mrs. Decker's first words were indeed in the nature of a bombshell.

"Ladies," she said, "you have chosen me your leader. Well, I have an important piece of news to give you. Dante is dead. He has been dead for several centuries, and I think it is time that we dropped the study of his Inferno and turned our attention to our own."

With all the power of her strong personality she painted a picture of the social and political problems which were troubling the world, and she made a plea to the women to drop their pleasant little essay-writing activities and to get into the struggle for a better civilization. Mrs. Decker made a clean sweep of all the committees, appointing able and energetic women to chairmanships. She created a few new committees, and to my surprise she called me from my place at the reporters' table to be chairman of the Committee on Industrial Conditions of Women and Children. She had had no direct contacts with working conditions, she told me, but she had read my articles in the *Evening Post* and she felt that the club women and the industrial workers must make common cause. Of course I accepted, and with the help of Mary McDowell of Chicago, May Alden Ward of Boston, and others who joined my committee, I set out to enlighten the club women. With the help of my colleagues I prepared reading lists, and through letters, circular and personal, I urged on the women the duty of informing themselves of local factory conditions, and of standing by factory workers in righteous trade disputes. . . . In 1905, with leaders in the Women's Trade Union League and the Association of Social Settlements, I was instrumental in securing the first official investigation into conditions of working women in the United States.

THE CAUSE OF THE EXPLOITED WORKER

Many of the first generation college-educated women were attracted to the problems of the industrial poor. Florence Kelley, daughter of a well-known congressman, took a degree at Cornell and then went to Europe, where she translated Engels into English. Coming back to the United States in the 1890s, she went to Hull House in Chicago and began to investigate sweatshops and to lobby for a factory inspection law. When such a law was adopted, Governor Altgeld appointed her factory inspector.

Florence Kelley was appointed Chief Inspector of Factories for Illinois in July, 1893. With a staff of twelve persons and a total appropriation of $14,000, she proceeded to make a name for herself and her department.

She was the first and, until Governor Alfred E. Smith appointed Frances Perkins in New York thirty-five years later, the only woman to head a state factory inspection department. The vigor and tenacity which had led her so far on her path, her moral fervor, and the training acquired in her social research had fitted her well for this office.

At that time (as, indeed, in too many instances today) the administration of labor laws had been the happy hunting ground of the politician, with labor department appointments distributed as political plums. Mrs. Kelley from the first regarded it as a serious scientific undertaking, the importance of which was unappreciated by the public. In later years she wrote:

A black chapter in our industrial history is this of our treatment of our factory inspectors; they have been left in the position of hostile critics, prosecutors—of corporations infinitely more powerful than themselves. Within the factory they have been met as enemies, bribed when possible, and in shamefully numerous cases, removed from office when they could be neither bribed, tricked, nor intimidated.

Under these sorry conditions the scientific output of these officials is naturally valueless. . . . Neither men nor women can do what needs

Josephine Goldmark, Impatient Crusader *(Urbana: University of Illinois Press, 1953), pp. 36–41. Reprinted by permission of the publisher.*

to be done until our whole attitude toward the task is fundamentally changed. . . .[1]

. . . As a responsible enforcing official, she now, in 1893, lived up to the standards she had demanded. Her four annual reports as Chief Inspector of Factories were something new in the dusty area of state publications. They are not like other official reports. In the words of two discriminating critics: "So moving and human are they, so full of indignant satire, so honest in their relentless description of conditions as they really existed, with no attempt to cover up or conceal the evils with which the state must deal."[2]

Child labor, sweatshops, accidents, judges remote from industrial life yet with power to mold it, all come to life in these vivid pages.

It is readily understandable that in her new position, Florence Kelley's experience and her own deep maternal instincts predisposed her to give a prominent place to the enforcement of the child labor sections of the new law. The conditions she encountered in the Illinois of 1893 were well calculated to emphasize this need. . . .

The number employed in the stockyards was not large. In her report for 1894 Mrs. Kelley lists 302 boys and 18 girls found at work there. But the conditions of employment then existing aroused her horror. That any human being should be subjected to such scenes and stenches was an outrage; how much more outrageous for young boys in their impressionable years. She had no legal power to stop these practices, but the public should at least know the truth. She would spare them none of the revolting details.

> Some of the children are boys who cut up the animals as soon as the hide is removed, little butchers working directly in the slaughter-house, at the most revolting part of the labor performed in the stock-yards. These children stand, ankle deep, in water used for flooding the floor for the purpose of carrying off blood and refuse into the drains; they breathe air so sickening that a man not accustomed to it can stay in the place but a few minutes; and their work is the most brutalizing that can be devised.

Mrs. Kelley's accounts of what she had found at Alton remained vivid to those who heard them at first hand. Many years later Alice

1. *Modern Industry in Relation to the Family, Health, Education, and Morality* (New York, 1914), p. 67.
2. Edith Abbott and Sophonisba P. Breckinridge, *Truancy and Non-Attendance in the Chicago Schools* (Chicago, 1917), p. 75.

Hamilton described the glass-house boys as Mrs. Kelley had made them live for the Hull House residents: "As she drew the picture we saw these little figures drawn from the orphan asylums and put in flat-boats and drifted down the river to Alton and sent into work as blower dogs, working by night or day, at any age they might be. She had been down there and seen them on the night shift and she had stood outside at the door and had seen the night shift come out, these little fellows trotting behind the men they worked for and going perfectly naturally into a saloon with them for a pick-me-up before they staggered home to go to bed." [3]

HELPING WOMEN WORKERS UNIONIZE

Grace Abbott was another woman who was associated with Hull House. In a memorial article, her sister recalled one of the exciting episodes in her long career in social reform.

THE GARMENT WORKERS STRIKE OF 1910

The Garment Workers Strike of 1910 was one of the great experiences of our early years at Hull House—the dramatic struggle of an oppressed group in a growing and successful industry. We knew many of the girls and their stories about their low piecework rates and their long hours. Everyone at Hull House was brought into close association with the men and women who were to form one of the world's greatest labor organizations, the Amalgamated Clothing Workers of America. We knew many of the girls who worked at night to make a living wage and others who took their needles home and threaded them at night so that they could work faster the next day. We heard them tell about the vest-finishing and coat-finishing, about the number of needles they threaded, the number of pants they made, the number of pockets and watch pockets, and all the rest of it, until Grace said that she could dream of pants and pockets and threading needles. Then suddenly

Edith Abbott, "Grace Abbott and Hull House 1908–21," Social Service Review 24 *(September 1950): 393–94. Reprinted by permission of the author and The University of Chicago Press.*

3. Alice Hamilton, speech at a memorial meeting in honor of Florence Kelley held at the Friends Meeting House in New York City, March 16, 1932.

came a series of walkouts—the great strike was under way—and, in a week, more than thirty-five thousand workers were out on strike. The strike began in September, 1910, and friends were needed to help the strikers raise funds for their new union. Miss Addams called on Grace to try to help her find ways of meeting the emergency. Funds were raised for the strikers, clothing distributed, and meetings were held—until the strike ended in January, 1911.

Sidney Hillman was then a new young trade-union organizer in whom the workers had great confidence, and Grace thought him a young man of great promise, who seemed to have outstanding ability and integrity. Writing of this period nearly thirty years later when he was recognized as one of the labor leaders of the world, Sidney Hillman wrote of her:

> I first met Grace Abbott during the memorable strike of the clothing workers in Chicago in 1910. We have met since on numerous occasions, at the birth of the organization with which I am associated —the Amalgamated Clothing Workers of America—and other landmarks. One occasion was during the most dramatic struggle of the Chicago clothing workers. Conditions had been intolerable; our organization had just then been launched—its treasury was empty, its friends few, the newspapers biased, the police hostile, the employers set upon its destruction—and the workers found themselves in a desperate conflict against formidable odds. Grace Abbott, then a resident of Hull House, together with Jane Addams and other prominent women, joined the fight. She joined our picket line, helped to collect funds for food and shelter, spoke at our meetings, presented our case to the public, and appealed to the city administration to arbitrate the strike.
>
> Grace Abbott had recognized the basic issues of the struggle and realized the need for the introduction of orderly industrial-relations machinery in the clothing industry, which had at that time just been making its initial steps and needed support and encouragement. Thus, back in 1910 and later during the strike in 1916, Grace Abbott helped to show that labor disputes are not private encounters between employers and employees but that they are of profound social and economic import and affect the entire community. She, moreover, helped to show that industrial relations must rest on a firm basis of better understanding and the extension of responsible labor participation in determining the conditions of work.

The unions were very difficult at times. Miss Addams tried hard to keep everything at the House pro-union in the letter as well as the spirit of union rules, but it wasn't always easy. Once when she had a difficult time about finding a new cook for the residents' dining room and the coffee shop, she got a Negro—a tall fine-looking man—who was a very competent manager as well as a good cook. The young Greek man and the Bohemian girl who worked in the coffee shop and also in the dining room liked the new cook at once, and everything was promising until Miss Addams wanted to have him join the cooks' union so that we would continue to have a union restaurant. He said that they wouldn't let him join the union because he was a Negro. Miss Addams was sure that he was mistaken; she couldn't believe that the unions were so narrow. Grace and I were both interested in trade unions, and Miss Addams said, "Well, we'll let the Abbotts see what can be done about this situation." But Grace was just leaving town, so that I was asked to "try to do something." I went downtown on a bitter cold, snowy day to see a woman whom I had known in the Women's Trade Union League, who was president of one of the women's unions, to see if she wouldn't help us. But she was uncompromising. "Why does Miss Addams have a Negro cook?" she asked very sternly. "Are none of the white cooks good enough for Hull House?" I tried to explain the difficulties of the Hull House situation. We needed a very special kind of cook—we were not a commercial profit-making restaurant—and this man was just what we needed. "No," she was firm; "when every white cook, man or woman, in Chicago has a job, then you can begin to worry about how to get a Negro cook in the union." I went home completely discouraged to report my failure to Miss Addams. When Grace finally got back and after she had had a conference with the union, she came home with a new and, as usual, very practical solution. The Negro cook was to join a Negro local in St. Louis, and Hull House would still have its union restaurant.

THE CONSUMERS LEAGUE

Josephine Shaw Lowell was a good example of a well-to-do aristocrat who gave her whole life to an effort to improve the

William Rhinelander Stewart, The Philanthropic Work of Josephine Shaw Lowell (*New York: The Macmillan Company, 1911*), *pp. 334–39. Reprinted by permission of Mrs. William Rhinelander Stewart.*

*conditions of life for poor people. Mrs. Lowell was constantly
searching for more effective ways to solve the problem of
poverty. In time she invented the Consumers League, which
became for a while a useful instrument for improving working
conditions. Her biographer described the way the idea developed.*

The bad conditions under which many working women and cash
girls were earning their living in the city of New York led them to
hold a series of meetings in 1886 for the discussion of these evils,
with the hope of finding a way to end them. Mrs. Lowell and her
friend, Miss L. S. W. Perkins, hearing of this movement on the
East Side of the city, attended one of the first meetings, and because of their interest and helpfulness, although not themselves
wage earners, were welcomed at the succeeding discussions to which
no other outsiders were invited and no reporters admitted.

Women of different trades and occupations told directly and
simply of their daily experiences, of many things in their places of
employment done in defiance of law, of the dangers, moral and
physical, amid which they worked, and of their fears of loss of
position, or threatened loss of character, keeping them silent, even
when to bad surroundings was added personal insult. These stories
were heard with sympathy and with respect for the stalwart and
upright views expressed, and for the high standard of honor and
generosity which characterized both the speakers and their fellow
workers assembled at these meetings. The helplessness of these
women to cope unorganized with the grave problems confronting
them, and without the force of well-informed public opinion behind
them, seized upon Mrs. Lowell at this time and engaged her lasting
interest. Out of these meetings grew the Working Women's Society,
organized in 1886, of which she was a friend and counsellor.

Being convinced that some of the existing evils might be remedied
by the appointment of women factory inspectors, to whom women
might freely speak of things they shrank from telling a man inspector, Mrs. Lowell was active in securing the passage by the legislature
of New York of the first law on any statute book giving working
women such protection. While the measure was under consideration, letters were received by Mrs. Lowell and others telling of un-
lawful working conditions; pitiful tales they were, of locked doors
in tenement-house factories with workers on the sixth floor, with

no fire escapes, and no water above the third floor, of narrow, unsafe stairs, of unsanitary conditions, and of insult. Mrs. Lowell was active and helpful, both with her time and her means, especially in some of the early strikes for improved conditions, and often presided at meetings, both public and private. No complaints were disregarded, and for many abuses remedies were found.

The work of the society continued, and in the winter of 1889–90 it investigated the conditions under which saleswomen and cash girls were working in the city of New York, and in its report showed them to be unsatisfactory in many of the large stores. Thereupon the society interested clergymen and philanthropists in the subject, and under their auspices was held a large public meeting in May, 1890, at Chickering Hall, on the corner of Fifth Avenue and Eighteenth Street, "to consider the condition of working women in New York retail stores." A report was made to the meeting by Miss Alice Woodbridge, for the society, embodying the results of the investigation and presenting the following conclusions:

> First. We find the hours are often excessive, and employees are not paid for overtime. Second. We find they often work under unwholesome sanitary conditions. Third. We find numbers of children under age employed for excessive hours, and at work far beyond their strength. Fourth. We find that long and faithful service does not meet with consideration; on the contrary, service for a certain number of years is a reason for dismissal. It has become the rule in some stores not to keep anyone over five years, fearing that the employees may think they have a claim upon the firm, or in other words, that they will expect to have their salaries raised. Fifth. The wages, which are low, are often reduced by excessive fines. Sixth. We find the law requiring seats for saleswomen generally ignored; in a few places one seat is provided at a counter where fifteen girls are employed, and in one store seats are provided and saleswomen are fined if found sitting. In all our inquiries in regard to sanitary conditions and long hours of standing, and the effect upon the health, the invariable reply is that after two years the strongest suffer injury.

It was the sentiment of those present at this mass meeting that the working girls themselves would be unable to secure needed reforms, for if they made complaint, others would be found to take their places, and that they were, as a class, too young and unskilled to make the formation of trades unions among them either practicable or useful. The remedy could be found by the organization of shoppers or consumers. The meeting therefore adopted the following resoultion:

Resolved, That a committee be appointed to assist the Working Women's Society in making a list which shall keep shoppers informed of such shops as deal justly with their employees, and so bring public opinion and public action to bear in favor of just employers, and also in favor of such employers as desire to be just, but are prevented by the stress of competition from following their own sense of duty.

Authority was also given to the chairman of the mass meeting to appoint a committee to sit with a committee of the Working Women's Society to consider and take action upon the subject. The joint committee decided to form an association to be called "The Consumers' League of the City of New York," and spent much time in the work of organization and in the formulation of principles. These were fully set forth in a pamphlet of some thirty-one pages written by Mrs. Lowell, entitled "Consumers' Leagues," and published by the Christian Social Union, February 15, 1898, in which she explained the situation of the working girls, and the objects of the League.

Employers may be divided into two classes: those who employ directly and those who employ indirectly. The direct employers, those who pay the wages and who seem to fix the conditions under which their employees work, are often as helpless as the employees themselves to change those conditions, because of the demands of the indirect employers. These last are the consumers, that is, the whole purchasing public, and, little as they think it, they have the power to secure just and humane conditions of labor if they would only use it. In order to induce them to use this power, it is necessary to show them how, and as a first step they must be made to feel their responsibility, must be made to realize that it is for the supply of their wants that all business of the world is carried on, and that their demands, however unconsciously to themselves, are actually the cause of the evils from which working men, women and children suffer. The rage of the purchasing public for cheap goods is the awful power which crushes the life out of the working people, and it is strange that men and women who would shrink with horror from buying stolen goods will congratulate themselves on buying cheap goods, one necessary element of whose cheapness is that part of the working time of other men and women, and even of children, has practically been stolen.

The great difficulty which has presented itself to conscientious individuals who desire not to take part in the oppression of their fellow men by buying goods made and sold under inhuman conditions has always been that of learning what those conditions were. It was easy enough for the abolitionists to give up the use of sugar and cotton, because these were known to be slave-made, but the conditions of so called free labor are more complicated, and in order to learn where and how the goods they desire to purchase are made, it is necessary to have concerted action, and from this necessity was developed the idea of the Consumers' League.

Early in 1891 the league was ready to begin operations. Before its formation, the Working Woman's Society had drawn up a "Standard of a Fair House," founded upon the business methods of some of the best firms in New York. This, with some modifications, was adopted by the league as the standard of excellence by which it would test all shops before placing them on a "White List," which was to contain the names of such retail mercantile houses only as in the opinion of the governing board of the league should be patronized by its members, and was to be published at stated intervals in the daily papers. At the time of the adoption of the standard, there were only eight of the large department stores in the city of New York apparently entitled under its rules to a place on the white list.

Printed notices had been sent to all the firms in the business directory of dry-goods stores, fancy notions, etc., asking if they would permit their conditions to be investigated in order that they might be placed on a white list and advertised as houses which treated their employees kindly, and approached nearest to the league's standard of a fair house.

REFORM IN LOCAL COMMUNITIES

Club women and other reformers in the thirty years after 1890 were especially involved in affairs of local government

Mary R. Beard, Women's Work in the Municipalities *(New York: D. Appleton and Co., 1916), pp. 56–58. Copyright © 1916 by D. Appleton and Co. Reprinted by permission of Hawthorn Books, Inc.*

*and local communities. In 1916 Mary Beard was able to write
a book on* Women's Work in the Municipalities, *in which she
covered eleven subjects: education, public health, the social
evil, recreation, race relations, housing, social service, correc-
tions, public safety, civic improvement, and government and
administration—all areas in which women's groups had been
actively engaged. The selection below is one small illustration
of the kind of thing Mrs. Beard was describing.*

INFANT MORTALITY

In this social battle to arrest and prevent disease, the campaign
against infant mortality assumes an even larger proportion, and
as we should naturally expect, women are also in the front ranks
here. More or less quietly for a long period women have studied
and worked on the problem of infant mortality. In addition to their
private efforts to reduce its amount, they have served in official
capacities. In 1908, for example, a Division of Child Hygiene was
created in the New York City Health Department, after careful
study of the organization of such an enterprise; and a competent
woman physician, Dr. S. Josephine Baker, was placed at the head of
it. It is believed to be the pioneer—the first bureau established
under municipal control to deal exclusively with children's health.
There had previously been diverse or scattered activities in that
direction but under the new plan all these were coordinated.

In Milwaukee, baby-saving on a "100 percent basis" was being
worked out by Mr. and Mrs. Wilbur Phillips when the defeat of the
Socialists brought their labors there to an end. Their experiment
was made possible largely by the financial and personal support of
Mrs. Sarah Boyd.

The combination of private and official activities in behalf of
child welfare led to the agitation of women for a federal children's
bureau to study infant mortality and nutrition. The scheme was
proposed by the National Child Labor Committee and supported
by the club women. Julia Lathrop was made chief of the bureau.

She was given a very small appropriation however. Furthermore
she was handicapped from the outset by her lack of satisfactory
records as a basis of work. "What do we know of infant mortality
when not a single state or city in the United States has the data
for a correct statement?" was her first query.

While pursuing the bureau's first study therefore, that of infant mortality, Miss Lathrop emphasized the need of better birth and death registration laws and methods.

It was soon recognized that women's clubs in the various states were the most hopeful agencies for bringing about better statistical records.

> The plan [of the bureau] is to have the actual investigating done by committees of women—in most instances members of the General Federation of Women's Clubs—who will take small areas in which they have an acquaintance and, selecting the names of a certain number of babies born in the year 1913, will learn by inquiry of the local authorities whether the births have been recorded, sending the reports to this bureau. An investigation dealing with about 5 percent of the reported number of births will probably constitute a sufficient test. The women's clubs are responding well and the work is progressing satisfactorily.

The recent Kentucky vital statistics law is due in a large measure to the women's clubs of the state, and the Chicago Woman's Club was also instrumental in getting a state bill for the registration of births.

The first monograph of the federal bureau was that on birth registration and this was requested by the General Federation of Women's Clubs. Other bulletins issued by the bureau up to the present time include Infant Mortality Series, No. 1; Baby-saving Campaigns—a statement of efforts made in cities of 50,000 and over to reduce mortality; Prenatal Care—a study made at the request of the Congress of Mothers which is the first of a proposed series on the care of young children in the home; A Handbook of Federal Statistics of Children, giving, in convenient form, data concerning children which had hitherto been scattered through many unwieldy volumes: a review of child-labor legislation in the United States and one of mothers' pensions systems. All of this information is of the greatest assistance to workers in municipal reforms.

While women in official positions are working to educate the public in child-saving, women physicians and social workers are constantly emphasizing the value of baby conservation at conferences of one kind and another. An instance of this among the many that might be cited is the participation of women in the meetings of the

American Association for the Study and Prevention of Infant Mortality. Dr. Mary Sherwood of Baltimore, speaking at the last annual meeting, said: "Communities and individuals must be made to realize the fact that the babies of today will be the fathers and mothers of tomorrow. Make the babies well, prevent mortality, and we have strengthened a great weakness. No community is stronger than its weakest point."

Dr. Sherwood is chairman of the association's committee on prenatal care, instruction of mothers and adequate obstetrical care; Harriet L. Lee, superintendent of nurses of the Cleveland Babies' Hospital and Dispensary, is chairman of the committee on standards of training for infant welfare nursing and problems that confront the city and rural nurses engaged in baby-saving campaigns; and Dr. Helen Putnam, of Providence, is chairman of the committee on continuation schools of homemaking and training for mothers' helpers, and for agents of the board of health, such as visiting nurses, sanitary inspectors, visiting housekeepers, and others. Included in the membership of this association are over one hundred societies which represent organized baby-saving activities in 53 cities in 27 states. Women are hard workers as well as scientific contributors in this association.

One of the most effective ways of stimulating the interest of mothers in educating themselves in the care and feeding of young children is through baby contests or shows or "derbies" as they are called in some places. One of the pioneers of this movement was Mrs. Frank De Garmo, of Louisiana, who organized a contest at a state fair there, and later, one in Missouri.

It was Mary L. Watts who so forced the better baby movement upon the attention of Iowa, through a contest for prize babies held at the state fair a few years ago, that farmers and their wives began to ask the question: "If a hog is worth saving, why not a baby?" Baby exhibits with their attendant instructions to mothers, whose pride and interest are aroused by the public admiration of fine infants, are now held from coast to coast.

A REFORM-MINDED PRESIDENT'S WIFE

*Eleanor Roosevelt, in defiance of her mother-in-law's ideas
about ladylike behavior, had been active in the suffrage movement and in the Woman's Trade Union League. She put this
training to use as the president's wife.*

Always, when my husband and I met after a trip that either of
us had taken, we tried to arrange for an uninterrupted meal so we
could hear the whole story while it was fresh and not dulled by
repetition. He had always asked me questions, even before the
Gaspé trip, but now his questions had a definite purpose.

After this trip he asked about life in northern Maine, and very
quickly the pattern for reporting on future trips evolved. It was
extremely good training for me, though my trips with Franklin
during his governorship had already given me some experience as
a field reporter. That I became, as the years went by, a better and
better reporter and a better and better observer was largely owing
to the fact that Franklin's questions covered such a wide range. I
found myself obliged to notice everything. For instance, when I
returned from the trip around the Gaspé, he not only wanted to
know what kind of fishing and hunting was possible in that area,
but what the life of the fisherman was, what he had to eat, how he
lived, what the farms were like, how the houses were built, what
type of education was available and whether it was completely
church-controlled like the rest of the life of the village.

When I spoke of Maine, he wanted to know about everything I
had seen on the farms I visited, the kinds of homes and the types of
people, how the Indians seemed to be getting on and where they
came from. I told him I thought they were of the same tribe as old
Tomah Josef, who used to visit Campobello Island for many years.
That interested him.

Franklin never told me I was a good reporter nor in the early
days were any of my trips made at his request. I realized, however,
that he would not question me so closely if he were not interested,

and I decided this was the only way I could help him, outside of running the house, which was very soon organized and running itself under Mrs. Nesbitt.

In the autumn I was invited by the Quakers to investigate the conditions that they were making an effort to remedy in the coal mining areas of West Virginia. My husband agreed that it would be a good thing to do, so the visit was arranged. I had not been photographed often enough then to be recognized so with one of the social workers I was able to spend a whole day going about the area near Morgantown, West Virginia, without anyone's discovering who I was or that I was even remotely connected with the government.

The conditions I saw convinced me that with a little leadership there could develop in the mining areas, if not a people's revolution, at least a people's party patterned after some of the previous parties born of bad economic conditions. There were men in that area who had been on relief for from three to five years and who had almost forgotten what it was like to have a job at which they could work for more than one or two days a week. There were children who did not know what it was to sit down at a table and eat a proper meal.

One story which I brought home from that trip I recounted at the dinner table one night. In a company house I visited, where the people had evidently seen better days, the man showed me his weekly pay slips. A small amount had been deducted toward his bill at the company store and for his rent and for oil for his mine lamp. These deductions left him less than a dollar in cash each week. There were six children in the family, and they acted as though they were afraid of strangers. I noticed a bowl on the table filled with scraps, the kind that you or I might give to a dog, and I saw children, evidently looking for their noon-day meal, take a handful out of that bowl and go out munching. That was all they had to eat.

As I went out, two of the children had gathered enough courage to stand by the door, the little boy holding a white rabbit in his arms. It was evident it was a most cherished pet. The little girl was thin and scrawny, and had a gleam in her eyes as she looked at her brother. Turning to me she said: "He thinks we are not going to eat it, but we are," and at that the small boy fled down the road clutching the rabbit closer than ever.

The pathos of poverty could hardly have been better illustrated. It happened that William C. Bullitt was at dinner that night; and I have always been grateful to him for the check he sent me the next day, saying he hoped it might help to keep the rabbit alive.

This trip to the mining areas was my first contact with the work being done by the Quakers. I liked the Quaker people I met, Clarence Pickett particularly, and I liked the theory of trying to put people to work to help themselves. There was a chair factory which was equipped with some of the most remarkable makeshift machinery I had ever seen, but it taught the men to do something in addition to mining and it also bolstered their hope. The men were started on projects and taught to use their abilities to develop new skills. Those who worked on chairs made furniture for their own scantily furnished homes. The women were encouraged to revive any household arts they might once have known but which they had neglected in the drab life of the mining village.

This was only the first of many trips into the mining districts but it was the one that started the homestead idea.

YOUNG WOMEN IN THE
CIVIL RIGHTS MOVEMENT

In the wake of the rapidly changing racial developments of the past few years, the Mississippi Summer of 1964 already seems far away. In that year nearly a thousand students, white and black, including many women, went to Mississippi to help black people register for voting and to organize schools among the children. Many of them lived with Negro families. Letters From Mississippi *published letters from volunteers to their friends and families. These two give some sense of how it felt to be a young white woman on that project.*

When any cars come here, Karol and I do a disappearing act into the back of the house. So far we've had no trouble. Sometimes around midnight when the dogs start barking we feel rather strange. Last Saturday night they started howling about 12:30 A.M. Karol

Elizabeth Sutherland, Letters From Mississippi (*New York: McGraw-Hill, 1965*), pp. 150–51; 195–96. Copyright © 1965 by McGraw-Hill, Inc. Reprinted by permission of the publisher.

and I turned out the lights and listened. The barking came closer and got louder until we heard footsteps under our window. The chase continued around the house while everybody else slept. Karol and I sat very still and listened. "I'd like to use the pot," Karol said, "but not with the Klan watching." The barking soon stopped and we fell asleep. Next morning, a neighbor came over looking for an escaped pig. We thought our prowler would have had to have been awfully short to pass unseen under our window. . . .

To my brother,   Ruleville

Last night I was a long time before sleeping, although I was extremely tired. Every shadow, every noise—the bark of a dog, the sound of a car—in my fear and exhaustion was turned into a terrorist's approach. And I believed that I heard the back door open and a Klansman walk in, until he was close by the bed. Almost paralyzed by the fear, silent, I finally shone my flashlight on the spot where I thought he was standing. . . . I tried consciously to overcome this fear. To relax, I began to breathe deep, think the words of a song, pull the sheet up close to my neck . . . still the tension. Then I rethought why I was here, rethought what could be gained in view of what could be lost. All this was in rather personal terms, and then in larger scope of the whole Project. I remembered Bob Moses saying he had felt justified in asking hundreds of students to go to Mississippi because he was not asking anyone to do something that he would not do. . . . I became aware of the uselessness of fear that immobilizes an individual. Then I began to relax.

"We are not afraid. Oh Lord, deep in my heart, I do believe, We Shall Overcome Someday" and then I think I began to truly understand what the words meant. Anyone who comes down here and is not afraid I think must be crazy as well as dangerous to this project where security is quite important. But the type of fear that they mean when they, when we, sing "we are not afraid" is the type that immobilizes. . . . The songs help to dissipate the fear. Some of the words in the songs do not hold real meaning on their own, others become rather monotonous—but when they are sung in unison, or sung silently by oneself, they take on new meaning beyond words or rhythm. . . . There is almost a religious quality about some of these songs, having little to do with the usual concept of a god.

It has to do with the miracle that youth has organized to fight hatred and ignorance. It has to do with the holiness of the dignity of man. The god that makes such miracles is the god I do believe in when we sing "God is on our side." I know I am on that god's side. And I do hope he is on ours.

Jon, please be considerate to Mom and Dad. The fear I just expressed, I am sure they feel much more intensely without the relief of being here to know exactly how things are. Please don't go defending me or attacking them if they are critical of the Project. . . .

They said over the phone "Did you know how much it takes to make a child?" and I thought of how much it took to make a Herbert Lee (or many others whose names I do not know). . . . I thought of how much it took to be a Negro in Mississippi twelve months a year for a lifetime. How can such a thing as a life be weighed? . . .

With constant love,
Heather

Dear Mom & Dad,   Holly Springs

It is a little easier working within the Freedom Schools but you still have . . . the pressure of a group of almost forty living fairly closely and the tempers and moods of your leaders and the guys in the field who sometimes find release for their tension by attacking others. . . . One of the hardest things is that you almost never have a chance to take a break. Sundays can be one of our hardest working days as everybody goes to church and some don't get back until late afternoon. . . .

Wayne's death exhausted all of us [Wayne Yancey, a Negro volunteer killed in an automobile accident]. Very few were actually close to him but his death was so useless and wore down our nerves. I think that all of us have felt in the back of our minds a little nagging thought that sooner or later someone would have a serious accident. Our project is responsible for about seven counties in northern Mississippi and we have had a number of minor accidents. The constant worry about policemen and hostile cars plus fatigue make the chances for accidents much greater. . . .

Love,
Pam

Carthage, August 9

I cannot wait to discuss something besides civil rights. Sometimes we make conscious efforts to discuss Plato or what's the best color for toilet paper—but it's useless. In thirty seconds we're back to C.R. . . .

Meridian, July 25

I'm a Northern white intellectual snob. I can't do anything at all about the Northern or the white part; I try (believe it or not) to subdue the snobbery; but I'm a college intellectual phoney by choice. . . . And in my short range of rather sheltered experiences, I suppose I have never spent this much time in such a culturally sterile place. . . . I got a letter from Dave today describing the most outrageous and absurd Mahler Cycle with which he was torturing our neighbors once again, and I must admit, the thought of listening to seven of those symphonies, more or less one after another, has never been more appealing to me. . . .

Dear All,   Carthage, July 14

Transportation is still our main problem. Farms are far apart—sometimes miles; roads are terrible, etc. One day Hank and I rode mule bareback. It was all I could do at first to hold on with my legs around his belly. . . . Soon I got the hang of it and did all right—didn't hold on or anything. Then a farmer gave Hank a horse and saddle, which he has been riding for two days all over the place. Talk about saddle sore, Hank the cowboy has to even sleep on his stomach. . . .

Love,

Judy

A BLACK WOMAN CIVIL RIGHTS LAWYER

Constance Baker Motley is now a federal judge. She says she has been too busy with the problems of discrimination on grounds of race to be much concerned with those based on sex, but in her own life she demonstrates once again the fact that

Peggy Lamson, Few Are Chosen: American Women in Political Life Today (*Boston: Houghton Mifflin Co., 1968*), *pp. 127–30, 136. Copyright ⓒ 1968 by Peggy Lamson. Reprinted by permission of the publisher and Cyrilly Abels.*

*a woman who concerns herself with effective reform often
provides a new model of what women can be.*

In Jackson, Mississippi, the newspapers called her "the Motley
woman." Constance Baker Motley had come to the state in the
spring of 1961 as counsel for James Meredith in his fight to enter
the University of Mississippi. She was then associate counsel of the
NAACP Legal Defense Fund second only to chief counsel Thur-
good Marshall; she had, for the past twelve years, been directly
involved with each of the Defense Fund's school and college segregation cases in the South; she had argued and won the first of her
ten cases before the Supreme Court of the United States. Still, in
Mississippi she was "the Motley woman." And in the courtroom,
opposition lawyers called her either "Constance" or "Motley."

One such unreconstructed Southerner, with a name straight out
of Faulkner, was Dugas Shands, the assistant attorney general of
Mississippi. On one occasion, in the course of the twenty-two trips
Mrs. Motley made to Mississippi for the Meredith case, she happened to meet Shands at the airport. He had been ill, and in her
friendly, natural way, she went over to greet him and to inquire
about his health. Unconsciously she extended her hand. Derrick
Bell, Mrs. Motley's young associate in the Legal Defense Fund,
was present. He recalls: "Her hand just sort of stayed out there.
But Connie showed no embarrassment." She looked at Dugas Shands
and then as casually as if she were saying, Oh, of course, I forgot,
you don't take cream in your coffee do you? she said, "Oh, that's
right, Mr. Shands. You don't shake hands with Negroes, do you?"

The line, especially as delivered, in Constance Motley's flat, un-
emotional voice, must have rattled Dugas Shands. He turned quickly
to Jess Brown, the local Negro lawyer associated with Mrs. Motley
and Mr. Bell on the case. "Jess," he said, "you tell Constance that
out here in public like this I can't shake hands with her, and I'm
sorry."

With a forbearance which has been characteristic of the Legal
Defense Fund staff, Derrick Bell explains the assistant district attorney's attitude. "Nothing in the Southern lawyers' background
could have prepared them for Connie. To them Negro women were
either mammies, maids, or mistresses. None of them had ever dealt
with a Negro woman on a peer basis, much less on a level of intellectual equality, which in this case quickly became superiority."

By her superb preparation, by her persistence in the face of over-whelming obstacles, by her straightforward, courteous approach, and by never losing her cool, Mrs. Motley managed, throughout the fifteen years she tried cases in the South, to put the opposition at a disadvantage and thus to triumph.

Now she sits on the other side of the bench. Her extraordinary composure is today apparent when, as Judge Motley, she enters a courtroom in New York's Federal Building. One quickly senses the poise and intelligence of this tall, handsome, Junoesque woman, although her judicial role does not offer much opportunity for the lively grin and the cheerful humor which have so endeared Constance Motley to her family, friends, clients, colleagues, and associates. Even from the bench her serenity is manifest. She has the calm of a woman whose sense of purpose has been fulfilled.

For Constance Baker set her goal early. She was a high school girl in New Haven, Connecticut, in 1938 when the Supreme Court for the first time in the twentieth century ruled on a civil rights issue. The case concerned a Negro named Gaines who had applied for admission to the all-white University of Missouri Law School. Since the separate-but-equal doctrine required the state to offer equivalent education to Negroes and whites, the university refused him admission but met the problem, as they had met similar ones in the past, by offering to pay Gaines's tuition at any law school outside the state that would accept him. Gaines challenged the constitutionality of the university's action; when the case reached the Supreme Court it ruled, in a decision written by Chief Justice Charles Evans Hughes, that the state of Missouri must provide an equal education for Negroes *within its borders.*

Constance Baker was an alert sixteen-year-old, curious, and interested in everything going on around her. Eager to learn, she went to all the meetings and forums offered at the local community centers and Ys. One evening shortly after the Gaines case a Negro lawyer spoke at the Dixwell community center on the significance of the Court's decision. Though hardly a revolutionary judgment, it was considered a wedge which might eventually open the way for application to racial issues of the Fourteenth Amendment's guarantee of equal protection under the law.

Listening to the talk that evening, Constance Baker made a decision about her future; she wanted to be a lawyer and to work in the area of civil rights. It was one thing to make the decision, however, and another to implement it. She was one of eleven children in a family of limited means; her father was a chef at Yale University whose salary could hardly be stretched to include college educations for his numerous children.

When she graduated from high school, Constance decided to work for a year or so in the hope of saving enough money to go to college if she could get a scholarship. She made her first attempt to find a job, and answered an advertisement for a dentist's assistant which stipulated that no previous experience was required. She phoned the dentist who told her to come right over for an interview. His office was three blocks from her house, and she left immediately. When she arrived he gave her a startled look; he was sorry but he had just filled the position. Constance Baker did not protest. She had hardly expected better, and, in fact, the only job she was finally able to get in New Haven was one with the National Youth Administration. Then, quite unexpectedly, after she had been working there for a year and a half, the entire course of her life changed.

One evening she went to a meeting at the community center in Dixwell, the Negro section of New Haven. The center had been made possible in large part by an industrialist named Clarence Blakeslee, who was present that evening, since the meeting had been called specifically to discuss why the Negroes in Dixwell were taking so little interest in their center.

Eighteen-year-old Constance Baker thought she knew the reason why, and she got to her feet and gave it. Negroes took little interest in the center, she suggested, because they were given no responsibility for running it. All the members of the board were either from Yale or were downtown business people. All were white. Negroes could hardly be expected to care greatly about something which was not really theirs.

Many of those present that evening thought that the girl had been rude to attack their benefactor to his face. Fortunately, Mr. Blakeslee felt differently. He made inquiries and found, among other things, that Constance Baker had been an honor student in high school. The next day he sent for her. He had been very much impressed, he said, with the way she spoke last night. Listening to her, he had remembered that Abraham Lincoln once said that God's greatest gift to the nation was an independent voice. He was prepared, he told the astounded girl, to pay for her education for as long as she wanted, to college and graduate school.

Happily Clarence Blakeslee lived long enough to see the end of a chapter in history which his protégé helped to write. He died in 1954 at the age of ninety-four, just after the Supreme Court ruled in *Brown* v. *Board of Education* that segregation in public schools was unconstitutional. . . .

For the next ten years, Mrs. Motley worked unceasingly to bring about compliance with the law in the South. In five states, Alabama, Florida, Oklahoma, Georgia, and South Carolina, she played a key role in opening the universities to Negroes. At the elementary school level she represented Negro children in twelve Southern and three Northern states. She worked in housing, transportation, sit-in cases, and protest demonstration cases throughout the South, representing, among other notables, the Reverend Ralph Abernathy, the Reverend Fred Shuttleworth, and the Reverend Martin Luther King, Jr., all of whom had been arrested in demonstrations.

During this period she was once introduced to an audience at Columbia University as a leader in the civil rights movement. When she rose to accept the introduction she began by saying, "I'm afraid I'm not really a leader in the civil rights movement. I'm just the one who gets the leaders out of jail."

Another woman lawyer and former municipal judge, Dorothy Kenyon, who was present that evening and is Constance Motley's admiring friend, wrote to her a few days later, "You get the leaders out of jail and their children into college."

Chapter 5

Women and Men:
Marriage, Family, Sex

The tendency of historians to ignore women has led them also to pay little attention to the social institution to which women are indispensable: the family. Anthropologists, sociologists, and psychologists write thousands of pages on the subject for every one ventured by a historian. Yet whenever the role of women changes, whether because of outside forces or by their own initiative, such changes affect the structure of family life and hence the whole fabric of the society.

Nineteenth-century Americans romanticized and idealized the family, but few students have tried to depict its reality. Such evidence as we have must be pieced together from fiction, biography, and statistics—for example, the figures on the rising divorce rate after 1870.

Most of the selections below are examples of reactions to real or imagined changes in the relations between men and women. These changes can only be understood against the background of what has gone before: the ever-increasing number of women at work for pay, the improved opportunities for education, the activities of the early women reformers. The boldest commentators called into question the traditional nature of marriage. Others took a new look at the responsibilities of motherhood, and the consequences for the society when the nature of the family changed.

THE CAUSE OF IT ALL

The fundamental change that lay behind some of the great shifts in family life and in marriage patterns was described by Edward A. Ross, a pioneer American sociologist.

As a boy I lived for some time in the family of a pioneer uncle in Iowa. His log cabin was a perfect fairyland for a child because of the fascinating industries carried on in it. Before the big open fireplace we passed many an autumn evening paring, quartering, and stringing apples and hanging them in festoons about the kitchen to dry. That was long before grocers began to purvey evaporated apples. Before the advent of winter great crocks of plum-butter and apple-butter were prepared, as well as jars of marmalade, kegs of pickles, and barrels of salt pork. In the smokehouse hams and bacon were curing, while in every corner of the cellar lay a pile of vegetables preserved under straw or dry earth. From the ashes in the great leach was drained the lye, which when boiled from time to time with refuse fat in the huge iron kettle outdoors furnished "soft soap" for the use of all save guests. Not only were there quilting frames and candle molds, but discarded in the attic lay a card, a hackle, a spinning wheel, and various other homemade implements, the use of which lay quite beyond the ken of a boy.

Now, at one time these industries were characteristic of most American households. Nearly all that was eaten and worn in the family had been manufactured by the hands of its womenfolk. In those days nothing was heard as to the "economic dependence" of the wife, of her being "supported." My aunt, busy in and about the house, was as strong a prop of the family's prosperity as my uncle afield with his team. Uncle knew it, and, what is more, *she knew* he knew it.

Gradually, however, a silent revolution has taken place in the lot of the home-staying woman. The machine in the factory has been slipping invisible tentacles into the home and picking out, unobserved by us, this, that, and the other industrial process. The knitting machine has taken the knitting; the power-driven sewing

Edward A. Ross, The Social Trend (*New York: The Century Co., 1922*), *pp. 78–80, 90–93.*

machine, the making of garments. The oil refinery molds candles for the household, and the soap manufacturer has made junk of lye leach and soap-kettle. The packinghouse has made the smokehouse a relic, while the store-blanket has relegated the quilting frame to the garret. The surplus milk goes to the creamery, so that the churn is becoming a curiosity. Canneries of all kinds crowd the grocer's shelves with preserved fruits and vegetables which formerly could be had only by the skill and care of the housewife. So, one by one, the operations shift from home to factory until the only parts of the housewife's work which remain unaffected are cooking, washing, cleaning, and the care of children.

It seems safe to say that *four-fifths of the industrial processes carried on in the average American home in* 1850 *have departed never to return.* What has been done with the energy thus released?

It certainly has not been diverted to rearing a larger brood of children. The first census of the United States in 1790 showed that in the whole population there were nineteen white children under sixteen years of age for every ten white women more than sixteen years of age. In 1900 the census revealed that the children and women in the white population were about equal in number. This means that the average woman today has half as many children to look after as had her great-grandmother. . . .

Observe, too, how it is nowadays between husbands and wives. When with spinning, weaving, knitting, churning, pickling, curing and preserving, the home was a workshop, the wife was not "supported" by her husband. He knew the value of her contribution and took her seriously, even if he did belittle her opinions on politics and theology. But, with the industrial decay of the home, it is more and more often the case that the husband "supports" his wife.

In the well-to-do homes—*and it is chiefly here that the status of women in general is determined*—the wife has lost her economic footing. Apart from motherhood, her role is chiefly ornamental. The husband is the one who counts, whose strength must be conserved, who cannot afford to be sick. Of course, much emphasis is laid on the wife's maternal contribution. But, aside from the one wife in six who rears no child, will wives feel and be able to persuade men that the bearing and rearing of three or four children offsets forty or fifty years of maintenance? Grandmother bore on the average six or eight children besides performing a hundred tasks which never present themselves in the modern household.

It is a cherished bit of make-believe that the husband is compensated by his wife's graces, her accomplishments, her culture, her social and public activities; that the "companionship" of so fine a creature is an equivalent for all she costs. But will nothing of patronage creep into the attitude of the breadwinner toward his unproductive mate? Having given up the role of busy Martha, is it not up to her to assume the role of the adoring Mary?

How will the case appear in the eyes of the wife? As the woman of leisure realizes that everything she eats, wears, enjoys, and gives away comes out of her husband's earnings, her rising impulse to assert herself as his equal is damped by consciousness of her abject economic dependence. She is tempted to pay for support with subservience, to mold her manner and her personality to his liking, to make up to him by her grace and charm for her exemption from work. This "being agreeable" means often that she must subordinate her individuality, hide her divergent wishes and opinions or adopt his. But this sort of thing dwarfs the woman, spoils the man, and revives just the thing we fancied was dead for ever, i.e., *male ascendency*.

So, although the surface current seems to be bearing women toward full equality with men, there is an undercurrent which runs in the other direction. Eleven million girls and women are outside the home slowly becoming vaulable factors in the working world. But within the home are more than twice as many wives, most of them constantly losing in economic significance. Will they emerge from their shelter erelong and find a way of reconnecting themselves with productive labor, or will more and more of them become passengers on a ship worked by the other sex? Certainly the cumulative effect of numerous small inconspicuous changes has brought women into a crisis on which turns the future of the relation of their sex to society and civilization.

MARRIAGE AND CAREER?

The question of whether married women could have separate "careers" hardly arose before the middle of the nineteenth century. In a rural society men and women worked together to keep the farm going, and in the colonial towns even women shopkeepers were still working at home, since the shops were usually in their houses. It was only as urbanization and industrialization led to the separation of home and work that the issue arose. (When women worked from necessity, whether they were married or not, there was no discussion of a problem.) In 1855 Antoinette Brown, who had managed to achieve her ambition of becoming an ordained minister, agreed to marry Samuel Blackwell, but on what were for that day most unusual conditions. She wanted it clearly understood that she would continue her career. Writing to him to explain her position[1] she said that she meant to work right on "without any change and compell the public to acknowledge me with at least as much favor next year as now. . . ." In answer to his query as to whether she was giving up much to marry him, she thought not; "Only leave me free, as free as you are and as everyone ought to be and it is giving up nothing. Relations will be changed but more gained probably than lost. . . . You may sigh for a more domestic wife; and yet to have me merely go into New York to preach Sundays, or gone on a lecturing tour of a few days won't be so bad will it . . . ?"

Married & still worked -

A PROTEST

Her friend Lucy Stone, another Oberlin graduate, agreed to marry Samuel Blackwell's brother Henry. They, too, took an unusual stand with respect to the role of woman in a marriage.

PROTEST

While acknowledging our mutual affection by publicly assuming the relationship of husband and wife, yet in justice to ourselves and a great principle, we deem it a duty to declare that this act on our part implies no sanction of, nor promise of voluntary obedience to such of the present laws of marriage, as refuse to recognize the wife as an independent, rational being, while they confer upon the husband an injurious and unnatural superiority, investing him with legal powers which no honorable man would exercise, and which no

Elizabeth Cady Stanton, Susan B. Anthony and Matilda Joslyn Gage, History of Woman Suffrage *(Rochester: Susan B. Anthony, 1881), vol. 1, p. 261.*

1. Letter from Antoinette Brown to Samuel Blackwell, December 14, 1855, Blackwell Papers, Schlesinger Library, Radcliffe College, Cambridge, Mass.

man should possess. We protest especially against the laws which give to the husband:

1. The custody of the wife's person.
2. The exclusive control and guardianship of their children.
3. The sole ownership of her personal, and use of her real estate, unless previously settled upon her, or placed in the hands of trustees, as in the case of minors, lunatics, and idiots.
4. The absolute right to the product of her industry.
5. Also against laws which give to the widower so much larger and more permanent an interest in the property of his deceased wife, than they give to the widow in that of the deceased husband.
6. Finally, against the whole system by which "the legal existence of the wife is suspended during marriage," so that in most states, she neither has a legal part in the choice of her residence, nor can she make a will, nor sue or be sued in her own name, nor inherit property.

We believe that personal independence and equal human rights can never be forfeited, except for crime; that marriage should be an equal and permanent partnership, and so recognized by law; that until it is so recognized, married partners should provide against the radical injustice of present laws, by every means in their power.

We believe that where domestic difficulties arise, no appeal should be made to legal tribunals under existing laws, but that all difficulties should be submitted to the equitable adjustment of arbitrators mutually chosen.

Thus reverencing law, we enter our protest against rules and customs which are unworthy of the name, since they violate justice, the essence of law.

(Signed),   HENRY B. BLACKWELL,
                                   LUCY STONE.

THE EFFECT ON CHILDREN

Hardly had the question of woman's right to work away from home been raised than the related question—the effect of a mother's career upon her children—followed. Four years after her unusual marriage ceremony, Lucy Stone, now the mother of a small daughter, wrote to Antoinette Blackwell that she had been to a lecture which had momentarily roused all her old desires to work in the great world. "But when I came home and looked in Alice's sleeping face and thought of the possible evil that might befall her if my guardian-eye were turned away, I shrank like a snail into its shell and saw that for these years I can only be a mother,—no trivial thing either. I hope you have a good sermon today." [1]

√ HOME AND WORK

Thirty-odd years later, Antoinette Brown Blackwell told a congress of women that it would be better for most women to spend some time away from home. Her suggestion that husbands take their turn at house keeping and child care was revolutionary in the 1870s and can still stir controversy in the 1970s.

So far from admitting that women have occupation enough in their family duties, I maintain unqualifiedly, that every woman, rich or poor, not actually an invalid confined to one room, is in imperative need of a daily distinct change of thought and employment. The change of mere recreation is not sufficient. None but very young children can find adequate satisfaction, or even health, in unlimited play.

Women need a purpose; a definite pursuit in which they are interested, if they expect to gather from it tone and vigor, either of mind or body. If their necessities compel this, let them seek for the stimulus of pecuniary gain, with the hopeful feeling that they can earn more abroad than they can possibly save at home. If one is unskillful and yet very poor, better to go out every day as a rag-picker, than to pinch and pine at home in unbroken weariness. Better turn charwoman and leave a six-year-old girl to play mother and housekeeper a few hours of pleasant daylight, waiting hopefully for mamma's return with a little hoard of luxuries as the result of her earnings. Two poor neighbors might help each other, one

Antoinette Brown Blackwell, *"The Relation of Woman's Work in the Household to the Work Outside,"* in Papers and Letters Presented at the First Woman's Congress of the Association for the Advancement of Women (*New York, 1874*), *p. 180.*

1. Lucy Stone to Antoinette Brown Blackwell, February 20, 1859 in the Blackwell Papers, Schlesinger Library, Radcliffe College, Cambridge, Mass.

superintending the children of both in the morning, and the other in the afternoon, that each family may receive a double advantage. Wife and husband could be mutual helpers with admirable effect. Let her take his place in garden or field or workshop an hour or two daily, learning to breathe more strongly, and exercising a fresh set of muscles in soul and body. To him baby-tending and bread-making would be most humanizing in their influence, all parties gaining an assured benefit, and the whole family might be expected to rest well at night.

The application of this mutual-exchange principle could be varied indefinitely. It might be made to abolish needlework, the present baneful method of eking out a scanty income. It would promote a cure of the hurtful sentiment, that the women of the family have a right to be supported; comfortably if possible, but otherwise that they must endure a meager fare inertly, to the detriment of all higher interests. Wives and daughters not only may starve rather than earn, but they still must do so or lose caste. Our "Woman Movement" is changing this sentiment, yet today ten thousand women would gladly be self-supporting if they could do so with no more loss of position than their brothers. Genius can make its own place honorable; but this seems infinitely harder to the great body of womanhood. As an alternative they double the time required in making each new garment, and quadruple it by altering over each old one, tempting their already overworked sisters into the same destructive fashion-seeking.

Women are in less need of more work than of a more sensible class of occupations on which to wisely expend their energies. To this end, also, we need a general reconstruction in the division of labor. Let no women give all their time to household duties, but require nearly all women, and all men also, since they belong to the household, to bear some share of the common household burdens. Many hands make light work, and hearts would be lightened in proportion. I would seek to have society so readjusted, that every man and every woman could feel that from three to six hours of each day were absolutely at his or her own disposal; and that the machinery of business or of the family would go on unimpeded meantime.

WORK AND MARRIAGE

Margaret Mead and others have pointed out that not only does every known society make some distinction between "man's work" and "woman's work"; it is also true that "man's work" is always more highly valued. It was this fact which Charlotte Perkins Gilman thought made marriage difficult for a woman. After marriage the woman was expected to become, in effect, a servant, while the husband went off to do the important work of the world.

. . . Each generation of men and women need and ask more of each other. A woman is no longer content and grateful to have "a kind husband"; a man is no longer content with a patient Griselda; and, as all men and women, in marrying, revert to the economic status of the earlier family, they come under conditions which steadily tend to lower the standard of their mutual love, and make of the average marriage only a sort of compromise, borne with varying ease or difficulty according to the good breeding and loving kindness of the parties concerned. This is not necessarily, to their conscious knowledge, an "unhappy marriage." It is as happy as those they see about them, as happy perhaps as we resignedly expect "on earth"; and in heaven we do not expect marriages. But it is not what they looked forward to when they were young.

When two young people love each other, in the long hours which are never long enough for them to be together in, do they dwell in ecstatic forecast on the duties of housekeeping? They do not. They dwell on the pleasure of having a home, in which they can be "at last alone"; on the opportunity of enjoying each other's society; and, always, on what they will *do* together. To act with those we love—to walk together, work together, read together, paint, write, sing, anything you please, so that it be together—that is what love looks forward to.

Human love, as it rises to an ever higher grade, looks more and more for such companionship. But the economic status of marriage rudely breaks in upon love's young dream. On the economic side,

Charlotte Perkins Gilman, Women and Economics *(Boston: Small and Maynard, 1898), pp. 218–19.*

apart from all the sweetness and truth of the sex relation, the woman in marrying becomes the house servant, or at least the house-keeper, of the man. Of the world we may say that the intimate personal necessities of the human animal are ministered to by woman. Married lovers do not work together. They may, if they have time, rest together; they may, if they can, play together; but they do not make beds and sweep and cook together, and they do not go downtown to the office together. They are economically on entirely different social planes, and these constitute a bar to any higher, truer union than such as we see about us.

BUT WHAT ABOUT THE CHILDREN?

Anna Garlin Spencer, another able woman who had given much thought to the problems of women and work, was cautious about the effect of working mothers on children.

. . . It would seem, therefore, that no economic readjustment of society in accordance with modern specialization of effort can make it possible for the average mother of several young children to pursue a specialty of work with the same uninterrupted effort that the average man can do. That all women should be educated for self-support at a living wage is a social necessity; that women should be made as valuable now and in the future as they have been in the past as distinct economic factors is unquestionable; that women must reshape many of their activities to suit the general scheme of industry which has created the factory is certain; that women should, for their own best good and for the ends of social progress, keep their hands on some specialty of work, if only in selective interest, through the years when they cannot follow it as the first obligation is clear; that women should hold in mind steadily reentrance into their chosen vocation when the children are grown, in order that life may mean for them continual flowering of the stalk as well as the past season's scattered blossoms—this is coming to be perceived as the wise plan for all women who would achieve for themselves, as well as help others to achieve, full personality.

Anna Garlin Spencer, Woman's Place in Social Culture, 2nd ed. (*Philadelphia:* J. B. Lippincott, 1925), *pp. 172–73 (first edition, 1912). Copyright, 1925, by* J. B. Lippincott Company. Reprinted by permission of the publisher.

This does not imply, however, that the physical exigencies and the spiritual demands of family life can ever be reduced to such a perfect factory system as to place the fathers and mothers of young children on the same plane of competitive manual and professional labor. The development of personality is the main business in life, our own personality and that of our offspring; to enrich the world with a unique contribution, made of the universal elements, but shaped to some rare beauty all its own. The old familiar faith, "God couldn't be everywhere—so he made mothers," has its modern scientific translation. The purpose of cosmic effort toward that "one far-off divine event toward which the whole creation moves" cannot achieve its personal work without persons. Personality is not the power to do any specific thing well, although vocational effectiveness is an expression of personality; nor is it a capacity to excel all previous achievements of the human race in some one line of thought or action, although great persons may also be great geniuses. Personality is above all the quality of unity, some individual wholeness that prevents the human creature from wholly losing himself in the whirl of things. To develop this, even in common measure, in the average life, it seems to be necessary that at the point when the child is first making effort to become a person there shall be some quiet brooding, some leisurely companionship of the beloved, a rich and generous sharing of some larger life always near when needed; some life not so much absorbed in its own individual growth as to leave it unaware of the stirrings of another toward more conscious being. For this reason, most of all, the individualization of women within the family may often be rightfully subordinate, so far as vocational achievement is concerned, to the development of that kind of personality which is effective through its breadth and its normal balance of powers, rather than by reason of its technical achievement.

ARE WORKING WIVES HAPPIER?

There is a peculiarly modern ring to an essay published in 1907 by a distinguished sociologist at the University of Chicago, W. I. Thomas. His book was titled Sex and Society, *and*

W. I. Thomas, Sex and Society (*Chicago: University of Chicago Press, 1907*), *pp. 245–47.*

*in one chapter he made the case for more than a domestic
career. Not only did he argue that women with an outside
interest would be happier, but he saw marked advantages for
their husbands as well.*

The remedy for the irregularity, pettiness, ill health, and un-
serviceableness of modern woman seems to lie, therefore, along educational lines. Not in a general and cultural education alone, but
in a special and occupational interest and practice for women,
married and unmarried. This should be preferably gainful, though
not onerous nor incessant. It should, in fact, be a play-interest, in
the sense that the interest of every artist and craftsman, who loves
his work and functions through it, is a play-interest. Normal life
without normal stimulation is not possible, and the stimulations
answering to the nature of the nervous organization seem best sup-
plied by interesting forms of work. . . . Interesting work is, psy-
chologically speaking, play.

Some kind of practical activity for women would also relieve the
strain on the matrimonial situation—a situation which at present
is abnormal and almost impossible. The demands for attention
from husbands on the part of wives are greater than is compatible
with the absorbing general activities of the latter, and women are
not only neglected by the husband in a manner which did not happen in the case of the lover, but they are jealous of men in a more
general sense than men are jealous of women. In the absence of
other interests they are so dependent on the personal interest that
they unconsciously put a jealous construction, not only on personal
behavior, but on the most general and indifferent actions of the
men with whom their lives are bound up; and this process is so
obscure in consciousness that it is usually impossible to determine
what the matter really is.

An examination, also, of so-called happy marriages shows very
generally that they do not, except for the common interest of children, rest on the true comradeship of like minds, but represent an
equilibrium reached through an extension of the maternal interest
of the woman to the man, whereby she looks after his personal
needs as she does after those of the children—cherishing him, in
fact, as a child—or in an extension to woman on the part of the
man of that nurture and affection which is in his nature to give
to pets and all helpless (and preferably dumb) creatures.

Obviously a more solid basis of association is necessary than either of these two instinctively based compromises; and the practice of an occupational activity of her own choosing by woman, and a generous attitude toward this on the part of man, would contribute to relieve the strain and to make marriage more frequently successful.

SOME COMPLICATIONS

In 1927 a rueful feminist, bloody but unbowed, took some of the myth out of the spreading view that any woman who really wanted to could easily combine marriage and career.

I am happily and, I hope, permanently married. I have no great creative urge but do have a direct antipathy to housework and a slight facility in other directions. I have no time or disposition for complexes, fixations, or inhibitions. And I live in a small town. It is simple, conventional souls like myself who must face the difficulties of "being modern."

The rural and small-town woman presents a unique problem. Our social organization is simple and primitive. Woman's work is as definitely fixed as is a squaw's and she does it as unquestioningly. There are no parasites. For example, I am the only woman in our small Illinois town who keeps a maid, year in and year out. There is no provision made for the nondomestic matron: no preschool groups, no trained cooks or nursemaids, and very few jobs.

I closed my senior year at college ten years ago as president of the Feminist Forum, with an address entitled "Why I Am a Feminist." At the time I was considered in our little group a Queer One, and a Dangerous Radical. Any one of you, nowadays, could sketch the outline of my talk. "It is not necessary for a woman to give up her outside work when she is married, any more than it is for a man to give up his profession. So many of the former activities of the home have been taken over by factory production that a woman who is content to be a homemaker alone, is stultifying herself and lapsing into the role of parasite. If children are borne (I can remember how I hesitated, just ten short years ago, to introduce this rather breath-taking possibility) the mother need not devote herself exclusively to the physical care of these children. They will

Edith Clark, "Trying To Be Modern," Nation 125 (August 17, 1927): 153–55.

admire her mental alertness the more if she uses her intellectual powers to the full and does not lapse into a mere Household Drudge. A competent nursemaid can give baths and supervise naps and meals, and a woman who surrenders a Career to Home and Motherhood, is making an unnecessary sacrifice to the shibboleths of conventional society." It sounded so simple—then.

Just the other day I told my present "competent nursemaid" to put the baby outdoors for her sun bath. I stepped out the door to feel the direction of the wind, and indicated the exact niche where the blanket and pen were to be put—a sheltered spot in the bright sun being often forty degrees warmer than an exposed spot. I dashed upstairs to pound the typewriter in pursuit of my extra-home job. After half an hour my sixth sense, which Competent Nursemaids have developed to an uncanny acuteness, led me to go down stairs and see the sun-bather. I found her shivering with cold, penned up, in the exact spot where the wind whistled its gustiest around the corner of the house. Our elder daughter, aged five, still rolls her black eyes with a gruesome fascination toward the water tower every time we go past, since months ago she was told by a C. N. that it was there the C. N.'s father had been drowned. The full details of attempted rescue and resuscitation accompanied the tale.

But to go back to seven years ago. I was a social worker in New York City. I was making $125 a month. My fiance had left a well-established business in this little Illinois town to make Democracy safe. When that ideal had been brought to its thrilling consummation his business awaited him. I surely couldn't support him on $125 a month. He could support me. His capital and ambition were both invested right here. The reason we were married was because we found joy in each other's companionship. I gave up my job.

How was I to "go right on with my work," and live in the same town with my husband? We have a population of 1,308. When winter comes a kindly old lady, a Seventh Day Adventist, comes to our door carefully holding a newspaper which she spreads down and on which she stands, "so's not to dirty your floor." She collects all the old clothes we have for the three poor families in town and leaves us tracts which explain the "Menace of Spiritualism" or warn us to "Prepare for the Bridegroom." What need have we for a paid social worker?

So, jobless, I prepared to lead the parasite's existence. Since the factory had taken away all my traditional occupations, I would just loaf and keep house. If my daughters will let me, I hope I may help them to escape the agonizing exhaustion of my first year's experience as a housekeeper. To cook three meals a day, wash the dishes, and keep our small house only moderately clean was to me desperately hard work. I tried to organize, to "use my well-trained mind to solve my domestic problems," but the endless minutiae, the sheer physical labor involved in sweeping, mopping, ironing can't be organized out of existence. Let no one deceive you, theoretical feminists. Housekeeping for the homemakers who do not employ domestic servants—90 percent of the total—is a full-sized job, even in this enlightened factory age. But my neighbors convinced me that I had started too late in life to learn their profession. They do their own washing and ironing, and buy perhaps one "good" dress a season. The rest of the family sewing they do themselves. And they do it all with an ease, with a pride of competent achievement that leaves me sincerely envious. For I loathe every phase of housekeeping except cooking.

Hence, I got a job. Not because I aspire to a career. (One of the bitter steps from youth to maturity is when one discovers that career material is lacking in one's makeup, that one's work is to hold down jobs.) I simply wanted to escape as far as could be from the exacting profession of housekeeping. I do newspaper feature writing for a small city newspaper. Because my father chanted the Iliad in Greek to us as a lullaby when we were infants, and because we attended the German Lutheran summer school in vacations in order to learn idiomatic German, we were known to the editor of the paper as a family of "culture," and on that basis he gave me a chance to run my department by long distance from our little town. I do not believe that every uprooted young wife would be equally fortunate. Part-time jobs for educated women may be developing in cities. They are few and far between in rural and small-town America.

A short while after achieving my job, small but precious to me, I became pregnant. According to the theorists, I should have given up my job for two years when I discovered my condition, or else have been such a thoroughly normal woman that the natural function of motherhood would cause me no physical discomfort. Neither of these things happened. If I gave up my job, just after having made a place for it in my life, I should lose it forever. Furthermore, I suffer considerable discomfort during the early months of pregnancy. Hence I would sit at my typewriter and pound the keys until a wave of nausea laid me low. Then I would stretch out on the bed and read the books from which I gathered my newspaper material until I caught my breath again, and then back to the typewriter. I managed to hold down my job and have the baby, and now, when I see her fat legs trotting around on endless weighty errands, I am sentimentally glad that nature triumphed over science.

But a job at what price! I have become of necessity a bovine creature who has foregone completely the joy of having nerves or temperament. There is not fifteen minutes of any morning when I work at my typewriter without an interruption. Our small son is going through the difficult transition from babyhood to boyhood. His present title in the family circle is The Prince of Wails or his elder sister's polysyllabic epithet, CryBabyCryStickYourFingerInYourEye. Bumps and hurt feelings have to be kissed away a dozen times a day. Our daughter in kindergarten daily brings home slips of paper with the information "The cat ran to the tree" repeated in wobbling characters over and over on a manila sheet. This herculean effort must be enthusiastically praised and cautiously criticized the minute she enters the house. I have yet to find the mythical nursemaid who regards sieved carrots for the baby as a different article from carrots mashed into hunks with a fork, or a sterile bottle as one to which a few flakes of milk curd may not adhere, or a teaspoonful of cod-liver oil as anything but sheerest nonsense. And after I have written down in black and white the day's menus and have done the ordering, the morning is blessed and unique when a plaintive, nasal voice does not call at least five times up the stairs messages running from, "Say, I fergot t'tell you, we was outa laundry soap," to a conversational comment, "Say, it sure is a swell day, ain't it?" Since I am the only woman in the knowledge of most of our neighbors who attempts to "hire her work done and write instead," as one of them neatly phrased it, my efforts are regarded by our townspeople as a mere pastime. When I started, I tried with as little pomposity as possible to let it be known that I reserved the morning hours for my newspaper work. A few blessed kindly souls still respect those hours, but the rest, now that the novelty has worn off, think nothing of running in for "just a minute" to get reading material for a study club lesson on Ralph Connor, the Preacher-Novelist, or telephoning to know whether I want to bring two apple pies or stewed chicken and noodles to the Fireman's Benefit. I have learned to switch placidly from reading "The Sun Also Rises" for my newspaper job, to looking up It Takes a Heap of Livin' in a Place to Call It Home for Mrs. Krumbelbinc to read at the Woman's Culture Society guest day program.

I left college with a strong sense of community responsibility. This was fostered by my years of social work after college. An opportunity for disinterested, intelligent community work assails my eyes on every side. I visit my little girl in the kindergarten room. One child sits dully in his little red chair with mouth ajar and eyes half closed. His condition calls aloud for tonsil and adenoid operation. Another little girl each time complains that her stomach aches or her legs hurt. She is pot-bellied and round shouldered—a perfect example of malnutrition. A Parent Teacher Association would bring a school nurse and supplementary food. I go downtown in the afternoon or evening. Arm in arm, up and down the main block of Main Street walk the high school girls, in the doorways lounge the boys. Dances are frowned upon by the school authorities. The gymnasium equipment is woefully inadequate. There is not another thing in the world for the young people to do but lounge and flirt in the gossiping eye of Main Street. Recreational facilities for the boys and girls of our community are a crying need. Every week or so two or three middle-aged men get together and saw away on violins. A crowd gathers on the sidewalk to listen to the old-time fiddling. It is the only music except for church choirs that the town affords. A grown-up singing school would be a joy-bringer. Three Protestant churches struggle along on a pitifully small budget. A united Community Church would bring to us here a well-educated young minister, and a well-equipped church plant.

Yet when these matters are brought up for discussion among the town's intelligentsia I withdraw into a frigid little zone of silence. I have neither the time nor the physical energy to undertake the role of booster for the most worthwhile thing in the world. By bitter experience I have learned that I cannot coach plays for the benefit of the library fund or solicit members for the Community Club, and at the same time write a decent article or be decently calm as a household administrator.

I shut my eyes to the books on the importance of the early years of a child's life. Aside from guarding zealously the physical well-being of my children (I can conscientiously feel that I am vigilant in that respect), I do not give them the companionship that a thoroughly single-track mother might give. (But I cannot see that the children of thoroughly domestic mothers receive much more direction.) My children do not know what directed play is. The words "Montessori system" have in their very context a syllable of reproach. I wilfully blind myself to the chance for rich and full development which the newer systems of preschool work might hold for my infants if I were willing to take hours of every day as teacher.

But in spite of hesitations, doubts, and questionings, I hang on like grim death to my newspaper job. My reasons are simple and selfish. My monthly paycheck is a welcome addition to the family budget, and a degree of financial independence is heart-warming to one who has tried the sentimental role of partner-homemaker with its uneconomic "allowance" dole. Housework as a life job bores and enrages me. Writing, even such hack work as I do, lights up windows for my soul. The idea of eventually learning to keep a clean house and bake good pastry does not inspire me with enthusiasm, whereas the thought of achieving even moderate success as a writer sends shivers up and down my spine. And last, through the outlet of the reading and writing that my job entails I am able to endure the lack of stimulating association of small-town life.

As for the children, time alone can tell the story. They have fresh air in abundance, the companionship of other children, good food, regular hours. Whether or not they will suffer from the repeated injunction, "Now run away and play. Mother must pound the typewriter," remains to be seen. I like to believe with Samuel Butler that perhaps they will benefit by it.

CAN A MOTHER WORK?

In 1964 Bruno Bettelheim told a conference of women at the Massachusetts Institute of Technology that working mothers were not a new idea, and suggested some social arrangements that might make it more feasible for women to work because they wanted to.

First let us discuss the erroneous idea that the working wife and mother is a modern invention. On the contrary, the full-time wife

Bruno Bettelheim, "Commitment Required of a Woman," in Jacquelyn A. Mattfeld and Carl G. Van Aken, Women and the Scientific Professions (Cambridge: M.I.T. Press, 1965), pp. 13–17. Reprinted by permission of the publisher.

and mother is a phenomenon that only modern technology has made possible. Before the industrial revolution and except for ruling groups of insignificant number, both men and women of all societies not based on slavery had to be active in the economic process if the family was to prosper. The pioneer woman, and later the wife of the farmer, the small artisan, and the shopkeeper was usually as fully involved in the economic and social activities of the family as her husband. The lives of both husband and wife moved within the small circle of village life in which both were an integral part. Their worlds were not separated, either socially or economically, or spiritually; nor was the world of adults set apart from children. Such a life was far from idyllic. Labor was cruel, life was full of anxieties, and amenities were few. But people shared it and were rarely alone in their struggle. Their very existence depended on working together.

If working for sheer survival formed the essence of life, then they had a full life. And this is what counts in terms of human satisfaction, whether the things we are doing seem to be the most meaningful things we can possibly do. If they are, we attain self-realization whether we call this human integration, or autonomy, or self-actualization, or an access to peak experience.

Obviously no self-realization is possible unless man has mastered his two greatest tasks: first, self-preservation, which in our present world includes not only preservation of the existing population but also extending the scope of our mass technological society; and, second, the procreation of the species. Of these two tasks the first has been more the domain of the male, the second of the female. At the same time, no full self-realization was possible for either sex without active participation in both tasks. Thus while man's principal means of self-realization was through work, he could not achieve it without his role as husband and father becoming central to the meaning of his life. Woman's parallel path to autonomy lay in being wife and mother. But unless she, too, had a meaningful share in the work of preserving the present generation and of extending the horizons of future generations, procreation alone was not enough to fill out the meaning of her life. Before birth control the more numerous pregnancies certainly made her fully aware of her procreative role. That she was also worn out by these pregnancies as much as by physical and economic hardships is here beside the point. What is significant is that only technological advances (less physical hardship in production) and scientific progress (control of pregnancies) permit both sexes today to find self-realization in ways they have chosen and not ways that are forced on them by necessity.

To a large degree the problems facing professional women stem from the fact that these women are expected today to enter a masculinely oriented working world as men, so to speak. They have all too little chance to enter a world that is at least as organized for the requirements of working women as it is for the requirements of the machine, or technology, or a science whose requirements are viewed as independent of the inner needs of the men and women who pursue them.

To remedy this we must start with the realization that, as much as women want to be good scientists or engineers, they want first and foremost to be womanly companions of men and to be mothers. In our thinking on working mothers the attitude seems to be that it is their motherhood that must somehow be fitted into their working life. Knowing that this runs counter to their natural desires, many women give up trying to fit work into their prime concern with motherhood. Well-intentioned efforts to encourage women to continue in their profession after their children are fairly grown only sidestep the issue, because they start with the assumption that the two—work and motherhood—are not really compatible. And they are not, unless work and child care are so arranged that neither childhood nor motherhood suffers.

A felicitous arrangement would require as a minimum: shorter working hours for the mothers of young children, work close to their home, excellent professional care for their children during the at-first four and later six hours these women would spend at work away from home, and ready availability of the mother to her children in the event of emergency.

Such arrangements presuppose an entirely different attitude toward work. They require that we free ourselves of the idea that this is still a life where we are just a hairsbreadth away from starvation. . . . Since the beginning of time man has lived in scarcity. Now for the first time, modern technology has done away with scarcity, or has the potential to do so. But scarcity thinking dies slow. Even while we busily plan for change, we persist in our psychological blindness to changes that are already fact.

Let me illustrate with the fetish of efficiency. It was the efficiency of modern technology that made us rich. But now that we are rich, we need not sacrifice to this god any more. We can afford to take our work at a more leisurely pace. If we do, we will not need to escape from work or fight for shorter hours or for more leisure time that we do not know how to fill. When labor is backbreaking, there is no point in stretching it out; the sooner it is completed the better. But labor need not be backbreaking any more. With monotonous work, too, there is no point in taking it more slowly; it only stretches out the hours of monotony. But labor need not be monotonous, if we do not sacrifice to efficiency at all cost. By using our full potential of workers, male and female, young and old, we could produce all the goods and services they could reasonably require. We could do it by making allowances for the need to humanize work: by making it companionable, unexhausting, diversified, and satisfying in itself, beyond the wages it brings. If we do this, I believe we shall also have gone a long way toward controlling the population explosion. Women who also find satisfaction in work will not have to produce large numbers of children as their only means of satisfaction. It is not the professional woman who sets six or more children into the world.

Radical as are the changes in attitude I am suggesting, they are only the first steps in the humanization of work that modern technology permits. They are only preconditions for the most important change of all: to arrange work in line with the psychological nature of man which, at different times of his life, is very different. Thanks to mass production and automation, we have new freedoms now, in arranging our work within the human dimension. These would permit us to change the nature of what a man or woman is working on, in line with the life style of his age group and sex. Most people find that the same work, after a number of years, becomes monotonous, however intrinsically interesting at first. They find new excitement in changing the nature of their work after the old work activity has gone stale. Also, there is work of a character and rhythm that comes naturally to a young person, and entirely different work that comes naturally to an old one. There is work that comes naturally to a young woman before she has borne her own children, other work that suits her best when her children are young, and still other work when her children are grown.

MARRIAGE AS A TRADE

According to the conventional picture, marriage is a vow between blissful lovers. But some critics, noting that marriage often provides a woman with her sole source of support, define it as a contract made for less blissful reasons than love. An eloquent statement of this point of view was published in 1912 by two well-known reformers, Scott and Nellie Nearing.

There is, however, another aspect of marriage, far too often disregarded, which is neither so idealistic nor so beautiful as the social and religious aspect. I speak of the aspect of Marriage as a Trade.

To how many men, I wonder, has it ever occurred that for the vast majority of women marriage was until very recently the only means of support in which they could retain the respect of the world? The "old maid" has been the laughing-stock of generations, the first and last resource of the comic magazines, the joke-makers and punsters. Men, from time immemorial have been allowed to choose their trade or occupation. Even the members of the proletariat may at least choose the method by which they shall be exploited—the manner in which they shall labor for their subsistence. But women, excluded from the field of industry, often barred by custom and law from even possessing property, have had but one choice. If the individual woman could succeed in so arousing and fulfilling the desires of the male as to induce him to share his property and earnings with her, she might by a simple process of exchange, yield up her person for the means of existence. Any variation from this rule in past generations met not only with the disapprobation of the world but even with persecution and punishment. Witch-burning, commonly thought of as a relic of barbarism, was in the last analysis merely the penalty paid by women who deviated from the type of colorless wife and mother of which men approved at that time. It was not only the hag, the decrepit and the infirm who fell victims to this barbarity, it was the woman who evinced any kind of peculiarity, whether unusual beauty, mental power or the genius of Joan d'Arc.

Scott Nearing and Nellie Nearing, Woman and Social Progress *(New York: The Macmillan Company, 1912), pp. 79–81.*

Is it strange, then, that women are eager to marry—that, after all other trades have been forbidden them, they cling to marriage as a first and last resort—their only hope of social salvation? Is it surprising that they learn to point the finger of scorn at the unmarried women? Far be it from anyone to cast reflection upon the bachelor! Moreover since the census figures tell us that females are in the majority in practically all civilized countries, and since a more or less fixed percentage of the men everywhere elect to remain in single blessedness, the mathematical result is obvious—a large number of women, no matter what their efforts or charms, must inevitably fail to enter the married state.

As a further handicap to the pursuit of her trade—marriage— custom has ordained that the woman appear reluctant to follow her compulsory pursuit. A strange anomaly! No other worker is subject to such a restriction. The laborer, the teacher, the professional man, offers his services to those who desire them, and is accepted or rejected according to his ability and the condition of the labor market. Unfortunately for women there is always a flood in the market of marriageable girls; and since any direct display of talents and fitness is forbidden, women have but one alternative— to wait.

THE MEANING OF DIVORCE

By 1912 concern over the rising divorce rate was widespread. Not every observer, however, viewed it with alarm. Anna Garlin Spencer, who lectured in social science at the universities of Columbia, Wisconsin, and Chicago, thought it might be an important aspect of women's emancipation.

Wherever and whenever the rights of women are recognized as those belonging to all human beings alike, there and then arise problems of marriage and divorce. For there and then marriage becomes a *contract,* and a contract can be broken for the same reasons that a contract may be made, namely, the good of the parties involved. The difficulties inhering in the adjustment of the domestic order to—

Anna Garlin Spencer, Woman's Share in Social Culture, *2nd ed. (Philadelphia: J. B. Lippincott, 1925), pp. 258–61 (first edition, 1912). Copyright, 1925, by J. B. Lippincott Company. Reprinted by permission of the publisher.*

Two heads in council,
Two beside the hearth,
Two in the tangled business of the world 1

are identical with the difficulties that inhere in democracy as a general social movement. Despotism is easy if you can secure a despot capable of holding his place. All else is a matter of adjustment to justice and right; and all such adjustment is difficult. In the midst of the confusion of ideal and action one thing is sure; namely, that women in the new freedom that has come to them in the last hundred years of Christian civilization will not longer endure the unspeakable indignities and the hopeless suffering which many of them have been compelled to endure in the past. That last outrage upon a chaste wife and a faithful mother, enforced physical union with a husband and father whose touch is pollution and whose heritage to his children is disease and death, will less and less be tolerated by individual or by social morality. In so far as greater freedom in divorce is one effect of the refusal of women to sustain marital relations with unfit men—and it is very largely that today—it is a movement for the benefit and not for the injury of the family. Permanent and legal separation in such cases is now seen by most enlightened people to be both individually just and socially necessary. Whether such separation shall include remarriage of either or both parties is still a moot question in morals. The tendency, however, in all fields of ethical thought is away from "eternal punishment" and in the direction of self-recovery and of trying life experiments over again in the hope of a better outcome. It is likely that marriage and divorce will prove no exception to this hopeful tendency. Moreover, so far as the testimony of actual life is valid as against theories only, the countries where no remarriage is allowed show a lower standard of marital faithfulness, of child care and of true culture of the moral nature in the relationship of the family group, than is shown in those countries that grant for serious causes absolute divorce with full freedom for remarriage.

That all divorces now obtained are for serious reasons, however, no one dare affirm. The most harmful element in the problem both in its personal and in its social aspects is the fact that selfishness, superficial and trivial causes of pique, of wounded vanity, of rash and childish whim, of even the mere suggestive power of newspaper scandals, may lead to a hasty and unnecessary termination of that

1. Alfred Tennyson, *The Princess.*

most important of all human relationships, the marriage upon which the home is builded. The special need, however, even at this danger-point, is not to focus attention, as is usually done, upon evils to be avoided in divorce laws and their operation. What is needed most is studious and practical devotion to constructive social measures that may be adopted for aid to those in marital difficulty, and for the prevention of those social and personal conditions which lead to marital difficulty. It is high time we began to work for the lessening of *causes of divorce*, for relief in family distress and misery, for helpful measures of discipline through recognized and adequate agencies for all who need an external conscience and an outside judgment to make a success of their married life. Not only is it true that an ounce of prevention is worth a pound of cure, but it is also equally true that a pound of help at the right time and in the right way to weak and ignorant and wayward people is worth a ton of prohibition. What many people need most is not to be forbidden a divorce, but to be helped radically in their lives and in their circumstances to a position where they will not want a divorce.

AN END TO SLAVERY

Almost two decades later Suzanne LaFollette, a liberal writer and editor, took an even more positive view of the subject of divorce.

The demand for easy divorce brings me to another aspect of woman's changing position towards sexual problems, and another cause of apprehension for the fate of traditional morality. It is a matter of record that the larger number of divorce actions are brought by women. Even if one take into account the masculine chivalry that often prompts men to allow their wives to pose as complainants, this fact still remains significant. Why do women take the initiative in seeking release from a contract that is generally supposed to have been devised for their special benefit? One would naturally assume it was because they found it unsatisfactory. Until

Suzanne LaFollette, "Women in the Modern World," in Johnson, LaFollette, Fishbein, Martin, and Leseman, eds., Civilization and Enjoyment, volume 8 of the Man and His World Series (New York: D. Van Nostrand, 1929), pp. 58–60. Copyright, 1929, by Litton Educational Publishing, Inc. Reprinted by permission of Van Nostrand Reinhold Company.

very recently, indeed, the woman who secured the benefit of marriage did so at the price of virtual slavery. Her property and her labor became her husband's. She could not engage in business for herself without his consent; she was subject to his will and liable to his chastisement; and she could exercise no parental authority over her own children, because, by law, they were not hers, but his. In short, she was, figuratively speaking, bound hand and foot and delivered over to such protection as institutional marriage afforded her. If she was discovered to have been unchaste before marriage, or if she proved unchaste after it, she was subject to extremely severe social and legal penalties. Unchastity, either before or after marriage, was regarded as exclusively a prerogative of men. To be sure, the Church enjoined chastity in men, and the State assumed it, but the terrible sanctions of feminine unchastity were not invoked against that of men. Such was the protection that institutional marriage offered to women before they began their struggle for emancipation. They accepted it so long as marriage was about the only profession open to them, or the only one for which, save with rare exceptions, their training fitted them. But as soon as avenues of escape opened before them, they ungratefully repudiated it.

The general acceptance of the idea of divorce at present is in great measure the result of woman's growing demand for reciprocity in her relations with men, and her refusal to be owned either economically or sexually. It may be regarded as an aspect of her general declaration of independence. That there are women who still make a profession of being owned, either in or out of wedlock, does not invalidate the general truth that as women have found themselves in a position to make their demands effective, they have insisted upon elevating marriage to a higher moral plane. Divorce has been one of the means to this end. No doubt it is a means often abused; but no institution has been more often abused by unscrupulous people than that of marriage, and no one ever thought the abuse an argument against the institution. It is largely due to the possibility of divorce that marriage now tends to be regarded as a voluntary partnership involving equal economic and spiritual obligations on both sides, and justly to be dissolved when those obligations have been violated by either party or have become onerous to either or to both.

That this change is not unattended by bewilderment and suffering is amply evident wherever one turns. It brings into sharp contrast the traditional difference in attitude of men and women toward the sexual relation: the leaning of women toward monandry and that of men toward polygyny. It is impossible at present to say whether this difference is more than traditional, and it will continue to be impossible until boys and girls are brought up with an identical view of life and of conduct. The woman of today, even though she is breaking with the tradition that has dominated the lives of her sex, has none the less been reared in that tradition; while the man of today is brought up in an entirely different kind of tradition. Only identical preparation for sexual experience would show whether men are actually polygynous and women monandrous, or whether both sexes are polygamous; or whether individual variation makes impossible the statement of a general rule.

BIRTH CONTROL

No single factor differentiates the family life of the contemporary woman from all women in time past more than the power to control her own fertility. Margaret Sanger had witnessed the miseries of slum wives as a public health nurse, and in 1912 became convinced that she must devote her life to making contraceptive information available to all women. Her publications were many times confiscated and she herself was sent to jail, though never convicted. Some of the court cases in which she was involved finally paved the way for relaxation of the stringent laws against the dissemination of birth control information, but it was a long hard fight. She continued her work in this country and abroad for many years, and in 1942 was made honorary president of the Planned Parenthood League. The following selection is from a book she published in 1920.

The deadly chain of misery is all too plain to anyone who takes the trouble to observe it. A woman of the working class marries and with her husband lives in a degree of comfort upon his earnings. Her household duties are not beyond her strength. Then the children begin to come—one, two, three, four, possibly five or more.

The earnings of the husband do not increase as rapidly as the family does. Food, clothing and general comfort in the home grow less as the numbers of the family increase. The woman's work grows heavier, and her strength is less with each child. Possibly—probably —she has to go into a factory to add to her husband's earnings. There she toils, doing her housework at night. Her health goes, and the crowded conditions and lack of necessities in the home help to bring about disease—especially tuberculosis. Under the circumstances, the woman's chances of recovering from each succeeding childbirth grow less. Less too are the chances of the child's surviving. . . . Unwanted children, poverty, ill health, misery, death—these are the links in the chain, and they are common to most of the families in the class described in the preceding chapter.

Nor is the full story of the woman's sufferings yet told. Grievous as is her material condition, her spiritual deprivations are still greater. By the very fact of its existence, mother love demands its expression toward the child. By that same fact, it becomes a necessary factor in the child's development. The mother of too many children, in a crowded home where want, ill health and antagonism are perpetually created, is deprived of this simplest personal expression. She can give nothing to her child of herself, of her personality. Training is impossible and sympathetic guidance equally so. Instead, such a mother is tired, nervous, irritated and ill-tempered; a determent, often, instead of a help to her children. Motherhood becomes a disaster and childhood a tragedy.

It goes without saying that this woman loses also all opportunity of personal expression outside her home. She has neither a chance to develop social qualities nor to indulge in social pleasures. The feminine element in her—that spirit which blossoms forth now and then in women free from such burdens—cannot assert itself. She can contribute nothing to the well-being of the community. She is a breeding machine and a drudge—she is not an asset but a liability to her neighborhood, to her class, to society. She can be nothing as long as she is denied means of limiting her family.

In sharp contrast with these women who ignorantly bring forth large families and who thereby enslave themselves, we find a few women who have one, two or three children or no children at all. These women, with the exception of the childless ones, live full-rounded lives. They are found not only in the ranks of the rich and the well-to-do, but in the ranks of labor as well. They have but one point of basic difference from their enslaved sisters—they are not burdened with the rearing of large families.

We have no need to call upon the historian, the sociologist nor the statistician for our knowledge of this situation. We meet it every day in the ordinary routine of our lives. The women who are the great teachers, the great writers, the artists, musicians, physicians, the leaders of public movements, the great suffragists, reformers, labor leaders and revolutionaries are those who are not compelled to give lavishly of their physical and spiritual strength in bearing and rearing large families. The situation is too familiar for discussion. Where a woman with a large family is contributing directly to the progress of her times or the betterment of social conditions, it is usually because she has sufficient wealth to employ trained nurses, governesses, and others who perform the duties necessary to child-rearing. She is a rarity and is universally recognized as such.

The women with small families, however, are free to make their choice of those social pleasures which are the right of every human being and necessary to each one's full development. They can be and are, each according to her individual capacity, comrades and companions to their husbands—a privilege denied to the mother of many children. Theirs is the opportunity to keep abreast of the times, to make and cultivate a varied circle of friends, to seek amusements as suits their taste and means, to know the meaning of real recreation. All these things remain unrealized desires to the prolific mother.

Women who have a knowledge of contraceptives are not compelled to make the choice between a maternal experience and a married love life; they are not forced to balance motherhood against social and spiritual activities. Motherhood is for them to choose, as it should be for every woman to choose. Choosing to become mothers, they do not thereby shut themselves away from thorough companionship with their husbands, from friends, from culture, from all those manifold experiences which are necessary to the completeness and the joy of life.

Fit mothers of the race are these, the courted comrades of the men they choose, rather than the "slaves of slaves." For theirs is the magic power—the power of limiting their families to such numbers as will permit them to live full-rounded lives. Such lives are the expression of the feminine spirit which is woman *and all of her—* not merely art, nor professional skill, nor intellect—but all that woman is, or may achieve.

A CASE FOR CONTRACEPTION

Mrs. Sanger worked with slum women in New York, at least in the beginning. In the 1930s a sociologist studying the lives of tenant farmer's wives in the South inadvertently documented Mrs. Sanger's case. Although the problems described here are made worse by poverty, the basic condition—thirteen pregnancies in twenty-two years—was possible among women of all classes who did not know how to control conception.

Here live the tenant, his wife, and nine of his children, ranging from two to sixteen years of age. His two oldest daughters, aged nineteen and twenty, married and moved away this year. Another child died three years ago. The wife is now carrying her thirteenth child, although this condition did not keep her from doing the largest part of grading the tobacco this fall. Her expressed attitudes toward her situation reveal some of the basic elements of tenant ideology and are clear from the following. She gets to feeling pretty bad when she's "that way" now, especially since she's had such a hard time with her last four—two doctors each time because they've had to take the babies ever since her twins were born. But she makes up her mind she just won't let it make her cross with her children the way some women are. And she remembers what the Bible says, "Be content with your lot," and tries to keep from worrying about not coming out even with the crop or about how they're going to feed and clothe another child. With thirteen children born in twenty-two years she has spent her life either being pregnant or having a baby too young to go anywhere. She gave up going to church long ago—or anywhere else. But she figures that you have to work and give all your time and energy to something, and she'd rather it would be to children than to anything else. Her two daughters who married this year never gave her a minute's worry and if

Margaret Jarman Hagood, Mothers of the South (*Chapel Hill: University of North Carolina Press, 1939*), *pp. 23–24. Reprinted by permission of the publisher.*

she can just live to see them all grown and married she'll feel she's done a good work. In common with many, many other tenant mothers, however, she fervently hopes that this one on the way will be the last one.

The worst thing of all about having so many children has been that she can't give them what they want and need. Take her girls fifteen and sixteen, now, in high school and doing well in their books. One of them is on the basketball team and they're having a banquet for them this week. This morning she said she had to have 80 cents to pay her share of it or she couldn't go and the other one said she had to have a voile dress because she was supposed to be a waitress for the banquet. There was one dollar left in the house —they had saved a little when they sold the last tobacco to have something to spend on Christmas and this was the last of it. And so the mother gave them the dollar together and told them to do the best they could do with it and to have a good time because it would have to last till next fall. "That's what's the hardest thing of all—having fine children and not being able to spend on them what you see they need." Yet this was said in a cheerful tone with no trace of irritation as the two youngest children tugged at her dress and interrupted in one way or another. Her countenance became more grave as she generalized her experiences to sum up the conditions of her class: "Tenants ain't got no chance. I don't know who gets the money, but it ain't the poor. It gets worse every year—the land gets more wore out, the prices for tobacco gets lower, and everything you got to buy gets higher. Like I told you, I'm trying to 'be content' like the Bible says and not to worry, but I don't see no hope."

A PUNDIT COMMENTS

In 1914 Walter Lippmann published a significant analysis of the political and social scene, including a perceptive discussion of women and marriage.

There is one question about feminism which is sure to have risen in the mind of any reader who has followed the argument up to

Walter Lippmann, Drift and Mastery *(New York: Mitchell Kennerly, 1914), pp. 234–39. Reprinted by permission of Walter Lippmann.*

this point. Does the awakening of women mean an attack upon monogamy? For the moment anyone dares to criticize any arrangement of the existing home he might as well be prepared to find himself classed as a sexual anarchist. It is curious how little faith conservatives have in the institution of the family. They will tell you how deep it is in the needs of mankind, and they will turn around and act as if the home were so fragile that collapse would follow the first whiff of criticism.

Now I believe that the family *is* deeply grounded in the needs of mankind, or it would never survive the destructive attacks made upon it, not by radical theorists, mind you, but by social conditions. At the present moment over half the men of the working class do not earn enough to support a family, and that's why their wives and their daughters are drawn into industry. The family survives that, men and women do still want to marry and have children. But we put every kind of obstacle in their way. We pay such wages that young men can't afford to marry. We do not teach them the elementary facts of sex. We allow them to pick up knowledge in whispered and hidden ways. We surround them with the tingle and glare of cities, stimulate them, and then fall upon them with a morality which shows no quarter. We support a large class of women in idleness, the soil in which every foolish freak can flourish. We thrust people into marriage and forbid them with fearful penalties to learn any way of controlling their own fertility. We do almost no single, sensible, and deliberate thing to make family life a success. And still the family survives.

It has survived all manner of stupidity. It will survive the application of intelligence. It will not collapse because the home is no longer the scene of drudgery and wasted labor or because children are reared to meet modern civilization. It will not collapse because women have become educated, or because they have attained a new self-respect.

But in answer to the direct question whether monogamy is to go by the board, the only possible answer is this: there is no reason for supposing that there will be any less of it than there is today. That is not saying very much, perhaps, but more than that no honest person can guarantee. He can believe that when the thousand irritations of married life are reduced, the irritations of an unsound economic status, of ignorance in the art of love, then the family will have a better chance than it has ever had. How many homes have been wrecked by the sheer inability of men and women to understand each other can be seen by the enormous use made of the theme in modern literature. It does not seem to me that education and a growing sensitiveness are likely to make for promiscuity.

For you have to hold yourself very cheaply to endure the appalling and unselective intimacy that promiscuity means. To treat women as things and yourself as a predatory animal is the product not of emancipation and self-respect, but of ignorance and inferiority. The uprising of women as personalities is not likely to make them value themselves less, nor is it likely that they will be satisfied with the fragments of love they now attain. Of course, every movement attracts what Roosevelt calls its "lunatic fringe," and feminism has collected about it a great ragtag of bohemianism. But it cannot be judged by that; it must be judged by its effect on the great mass of women who, half-consciously for the most part, are seeking not a new form of studio and café life, but a readjustment to work and love and interest. There is among them, so far as I can see, no indication of any desire for an impressionistic sexual career.

To be sure they don't treat a woman who has had relations out of marriage as if she were a leper. They are not inclined to visit upon the offspring of illegitimacy the curse of patriarchal Judea. But so far as their own demands go they are set in overwhelming measure upon greater sexual sincerity. They are, if anything, too stern in their morality and, perhaps, too naive. But the legislation they initiate, the books they write, look almost entirely to the establishment of a far more enduring and intelligently directed family.

The effect of the woman's movement will accumulate with the generations. The results are bound to be so far-reaching that we can hardly guess them today. For we are tapping a reservoir of possibilities when women begin to use not only their generalized womanliness but their special abilities. For the child it means, as I have tried to suggest, a change in the very conditions where the property sense is aggravated and where the need for authority and individual assertiveness is built up. The greatest obstacles to a cooperative civilization are under fire from the feminists. Those obstacles today are more than anything else a childhood in which the antisocial impulses are fixed. The awakening of women points straight to the discipline of cooperation. And so it is laying the real foundations for the modern world.

For understand that the forms of cooperation are of precious little value without a people trained to use them. The old family with its dominating father, its submissive and amateurish mother produced inevitably men who had little sense of a common life, and women who were jealous of an enlarging civilization. It is this that feminism comes to correct, and that is why its promise reaches far beyond the present bewilderment.

co - operation between men & women

WOMEN AND VIRTUE

Who knows when the "sexual revolution" began? Contemporaries labeled the last decade of the nineteenth century the Gay Nineties; Greenwich Village began to develop its bohemian culture before the First World War; and in the 1920s the trends were alarming, at least from the point of view of people over thirty. Here a young woman philosophy professor at Barnard College discusses situation ethics and the changing sexual behavior of young women in 1924.

The sex relations of an individual should no more be subjected to social regulation than his friendships. There is indeed a closely related matter for which he is immediately responsible to society— that is the welfare of any children resulting from such relations. The two matters are, however, quite distinguishable and no one could hold that the effort which society makes to control sex relations is to any extent based upon concern for the welfare of possible offspring. If this were so, one would not hear so much condemnation of birth-control measures on the ground that they "encourage immorality." No. It is personal experience which society would like to prescribe for its members, personal virtue that it would like to mold for them. But virtue is not a predetermined result, a kind of spiritual dessert that any one can cook up who will follow with due care the proper ethical receipt. It is, on the contrary, something which is never twice alike; something which appears in ever new and lovely forms as the fruit of harmoniously developed elements in a unique character complex. Experience cannot be defined in terms of external circumstances and bodily acts and thus judged as absolutely good or bad. Sex experiences, like other experiences, can be judged

Isobel Leavenworth, "Virtue for Women," in Frieda Kircheway, Our Changing Morality (New York: Albert and Charles Boni, Inc., 1924), pp. 100–3. Reprinted by permission of the publisher.

of only on the basis of the part which they play in the creative drama of the individual soul. There are as many possibilities for successful sex life as there are men and women in the world. A significant single standard can be attained only through the habit of judging every case, man or woman, in the light of the character of the individual and of the particular circumstances in which he or she is placed.

From the changes taking place in sex morality we may, with sufficient wisdom and courage, win inestimable gains. Certainly we should be grateful that young people are forming the habit of meeting this old problem in a quite new way—that is, with the cooperation of the two sexes. In the interest of this newer approach we should accord to girls as much freedom from immediate supervision as we have always given to boys. The old restrictions, imposed upon girls alone, imply, of course, the double standard with all its attendant evils; imply the placid acceptance of two essentially different systems of value; imply the preference for physical purity over personal responsibility and true moral development. We should encourage the daughters of today in their fast-developing scorn for the "respect" which our feminine predecessors thought was their due— a respect which man was expected to reveal in the habit of keeping the nice woman untouched by certain rather conspicuous elements, interests, and activities in his own life. In so far as there is something truly gay in these aspects of life, something which men know at the bottom of their hearts they should not be called on to forego, there is much that women can learn. Most people today hold in their minds an image of two worlds—one of gayety and freedom, the other of morality. It is because gayety and morality are thus divorced that gayety becomes sordidness, morality dreariness. Not until men and women develop together the legitimate interests which both of these worlds satisfy will the present inconsistency and hypocrisy be done away with and both men and women be free to achieve, if they can, rich and unified personal lives.

WHO SHOULD ENJOY SEX?

One part of the nineteenth-century idealization of woman and home was the assumption that the enjoyment of sex was only for men. Many women emerging into more active lives had grown up in this belief, with consequent problems when

*they discovered a conflict between their own experience and
what they had been taught. Here one woman, writing in the
Nation's series on "These Modern Women" described her
own experience.*

As long as I believed, in harmony with my early teaching, that
sex was a degrading and disgusting phenomenon which men enjoyed
but to which women submitted only because it was a part of wifely
duty, the appeal of celibacy and independence was enhanced. But
with the biology and psychology courses of college and university,
sex took on a new meaning. It was probably as much of a shock to
me to learn that women had their share of the sexual instincts and
emotions as it was to many of my classmates to come into contact
with philosophical doubts concerning the religious views which they
had unquestioningly accepted. My own churchgoing had been at a
minimum, indulged in purely at my own whim and inclination, so
that I was able to slough off what little superstition I had acquired
without any sense of discomfort. But to readjust my ideas and my
philosophy to a world which had suddenly lost its feminine integrity,
and in which women needed men even as men needed women, was
a serious matter.

It took many hours and days of reading to furnish me with a
background against which I could evolve a new philosophy to settle
this conflict. Westermarck, Crawley, Freud, Adler, Jung, Havelock
Ellis, and Ellen Key became my daily familiars. At last I emerged
with a modified viewpoint. The necessity of a normal sex life for
women was a scientific fact, and I must bow to the truths established
by science. I was not, however, compelled to accept the institution
of marriage, which was plainly a lineal descendant of primitive rites
and ceremonials having its beginnings in ideas of magic later carried
over into the folkways and mores. I could recognize that I had
normal sex emotions but I need not give up my freedom and independence by submitting to any such religious or legal ceremony. By
this formula, I was able to preserve my guiding fiction intact.

It is amusing, now, to look back on this process of reassurance.
Men and women are inevitably possessed of a power over each other
which cannot be thought out of existence or evaded by refusing to
legalize a relationship. Whether or not it is conventionalized, love

[*Phyllis Blanchard*], *"The Long Journey,"* Nation *124 (April 27, 1927): 472–73.*

has a coercive effect upon individual behavior; refusal of marriage cannot alter this fact. My fine theories, which were only attempts to effect a reconciliation of my natural longing for love with my desire for personal autonomy, never stood the test of experience. Once or twice I was tempted to relinquish my profession for the ancient position of woman as wife, but the spirit of independence was too strong. I might play with the idea of submission to masculine authority, but at the first sign of any real or permanent enslavement I shrank away and clung to my liberty. There was always my work to stabilize me in these crises. And as steadily as if there had been no such thing in the world as unsatisfied emotions, I won professional advancement. The loss of dear companionship could be forgotten after a time, in the world of books waiting to be read or to be written; my feelings were eased tremendously by writing.

The long struggle between my own two greatest needs—the need for love and the need for independence—probably had its effect upon my final choice of a profession. I had originally intended to write, but the drive to understand human motives and conduct, which arose out of the necessity of solving my own problems, developed into a desire to understand all behavior, and I turned to the social sciences. Probably this was a happy decision. Had I been only a writer, I might have prolonged indefinitely my separation from reality. Through a more scientific approach, I began to see things as they actually were rather than as I wished them to be. I even came to understand that in spite of the intensity of my feeling about marriage I might be able to accept the outward form so long as the inner spirit of the relationship embodied freedom. Thus, at thirty, I went forth to meet the fate which I had so long feared—and found it good!

It is fortunate for me that this venture has been with a man of insight, imagination, and humor, who cherishes no desire to be owner or tyrant. He respects my work as much as I do his. If he does not feel quite so keenly as I the need of economic independence after marriage, he is more eager that I have leisure for creative work than I am myself. Nor is this because my writings bear witness that I am his wife, for I keep my own name. To us, marriage is no sacred bond which it would be sacrilege to sever. Rather, we regard it as a form to which we have submitted because it is the only way in which we can give expression to our love without interference. With marriage, thus interpreted, I am content. It is as if I had accomplished the impossible feat of eating my cake and having it—for I have both love and freedom, which once seemed to me such incompatible bedfellows.

DOWN WITH THE MONOGAMOUS FAMILY

From time to time a commentator cut through all the talk about women inside and outside the home to say that the fatal institution, for women, was monogamous marriage and that either it was vanishing or it should vanish. One such commentator was the Marxist sociologist, V. F. Calverton.

When John B. Watson predicts that "the present marriage system (of monogamy) will end in fifty years," what he is really saying is that women are ending the system of marriage that men began. The Reverend Dr. Caleb R. Stetson, in describing the direction toward which we are now tending as that of "progressive polygamy and respectable promiscuity," is merely making a similar reflection upon the effects of this revolt on the part of women.

But such statements, which are to be heard on every side today, are less conclusive testimony as to the actual behaviour of women than studies of a more concrete and statistical variety. Among 1,000 unmarried women studied by Dr. Katharine Bement Davis, only 288 denied having had any sexual experience whatsoever. What does this study reveal? Simply this: that only three in every ten of these unmarried women were innocent of all sexual experience. The myth of the pure woman is almost at an end.

Among the 1,000 women studied, 730 admitted that they practised birth control, and while others were less candid in their remarks, only 78 expressed disapproval of it. This attitude towards birth-control methods is closely linked, as we observed before, with woman's new independence in sexual expression.

More interesting even than these statistics are those tabulated by Dr. G. V. Hamilton and Kenneth MacGowan in their study of 100 married men and 100 married women. Forty-one of these married women had outside love affairs, while only 29 of the husbands had

V. F. Calverton, "Are Women Monogamous?" in V. F. Calverton and Samuel D. Schmalhousen, Woman's Coming of Age (New York: Horace Liveright, Inc., 1931), pp. 484–85. Reprinted by permission of the publisher.

such affairs. What we have here is a definite testimony to woman's new behaviour. Here are married women, still living with their husbands, who are at the same time having love affairs with other men to complement their emotional experience. There was a time when this Madame Bovary reaction was singular. Today it has become common. Women are increasingly discontented with their husbands. Divorces demanded by women represent one revolt of the female sex against the old, lifelong monogamy. Their extramarital affairs represent an even more recent and more definitely antimonogamous tendency.

Anyone who is intimately acquainted with other studies in this field, in particular with the work of Judge Ben Lindsey and the revolt of modern youth, and who is at the same time aware of the actual behaviour of men and women as reported by their own words, by newspapers, and by courts, realises that the statistics given above are but a mild indication of what is already a deep-rooted trend. The monogamy of women depended upon the success of the family and the home; but both institutions, as even the conservative critic admits, are today in a state of disorganisation and decay. The rigid regulations which once held women in check have lost their old power.

As Alyse Gregory has pointed out ("The Changing Morality of Women," *Current History*), the girl now sows her wild oats as well as the boy, for "her employer asks no questions as to her life outside the office. She has her own salary at the end of the month, and asks no other recompense from her lover but his love and companionship." She is no longer dependent upon her family for her livelihood —nor, in many instances, when she is married, is she dependent upon her husband.

It is no wonder, then, that women have already begun to announce their revolt against monogamy. They are now able to be as free in the expression of their emotions as men. The right to love and to be loved has become a dominant force in their lives; the influence of respectability has begun to recede. Women are seldom terrified any longer by custom, or by the awful eye of the moral censor, which they now recognise as man's ambassador. They are coming to see— what man has always seen—that love and monogamy have almost always been historical contradictions. Except for occasional periods, fidelity has seldom been one of man's virtues.

THE FAMILY IN AMERICA: 1947

Just as the twentieth century approached its midpoint, a sociologist paused to sum up what he had observed about the American family.

If there is any modal type of family in America, it is the semi-patriarchal form in which a dominant husband "brings in the bacon" and a submissive woman plays a traditional wife-and-mother role. Child-rearing and homemaking are primarily the responsibility of the wife, whereas the business contacts and political activities of the family remain within the husband's province. This arrangement, midway between the familistic-patriarchal and the person-centered democratic family, is constantly being challenged by insurgent mothers who rebel against the confining role of wife-and-mother and by a few fathers who feel strongly that it takes two to make a home! In spite of the dissidents it is our impression that the family form is stabilizing temporarily, at least, at this point on the continuum.

Our cultural definitions continue to differentiate between masculine and feminine roles. The ladylike role shall be overtly subordinate, polite, and gracious. A manlike role must include self-assertion, initiative, and decisiveness. Many of our first- and second-generation immigrant families have never known any form except the patriarchal; for them the complementary roles of dominant father–submissive mother are culturally set. Moreover, in census-taking and all official matters, the national, state, and local governments provide that the family head shall be the husband, if he is living. The law further supports the semipatriarchal arrangement in delineating the duty of the husband to support his wife and children and the wife's right to exact support. No wife has ever been jailed for nonsupport. From the Hebrews down to the present, religion has supported the familistic-patriarchal form. In a text for Catholic college students the official point of view of the Roman Catholic church is stated in forthright terms: "The man is the head,

Reuben Hill, "The American Family: Problem or Solution?" American Journal of Sociology 53 (July 1947): 125–30. *Reprinted by permission of the University of Chicago Press, and the author.*

and the wife the heart of the home. . . . The place of the woman is in the home." [1] Among the authoritarian religions there is little support for the person-centered democratic family. Our scriptural exhortations leave no doubt where the seat of family authority should be. Even heaven is thought to be ruled by an authoritarian father.

Furthermore, money is a source of power which supports male dominance in the family. Unconsciously, the most emancipated of women catch themselves saying, "I hate to spend his money." Money belongs to him who earns it, not to her who spends it, since he who earns it may withhold it. When the power of money is added to the cultural definition, it is no wonder that equalitarian arrangements give way to the culturally defined semipatriarchal system. As more wives become competent to earn their living and choose that alternative throughout the family cycle, the power of money may be equalized between husband and wife. Meanwhile, even where both are working, the wife is usually paid less and her contribution is viewed as minor.

Finally, there is the mating gradient, a demonstrable tendency for men to insure themselves a semipatriarchal authority by marrying mates of less education, younger, and less qualified to make decisions. Thus are husbands prepared to dominate the family intellectually. Moreover, if their quarrels ever came to blows, his greater strength, physically, would settle things.

Person-centered democratic family living requires a skill and understanding now possessed by few couples. Mature, equally matched personalities with rich experiences in give-and-take are needed to found such a family. Neurotic, egocentric, domineering, and submissive persons are handicapped. The so-called "companionship" family appears to have much in common with the beautiful ideal of the "Brotherhood of Man" as a millennial goal. Both may well be desirable, but they are extremes based largely on the opposite of what is found in society at this time.

A more pragmatic approach is to examine the weaknesses and strengths of American families today and to attempt to formulate a national policy which would enable them to make the most of the challenging changes ahead in government, industry, and social relations. It is to that task that social science and technology must turn.

1. Edgar Schmiedeler, *Marriage and the Family* (New York: McGraw-Hill Book Co., Inc., 1946), p. 118.

A vital role awaits these disciplines, if not in changing family form or in creating new standards, at least in predicting significant trends and in adding to the knowledge of human conduct. We see the family, then, with these aids, surviving the present spurt of machine-age developments (our foresight does not carry us into the atomic age), of urbanization, of social mobility, of wars and economic depressions, with a minimum of scars and a maximum of vitality. We see great possibilities in the family of tomorrow as an improved small-family organization, geared to assure maximum self-expression of family members while maintaining integrity and inner loyalty to the whole.

THE RISE OF THE "FEMININE MYSTIQUE"

In the years immediately after World War II the United States experienced a new period of romanticised domesticity. Rosie the Riveter gave up her job to a returning veteran, and the government girls in Washington went home to marry the men who had fought the war. For fifteen years the ladies' magazines painted an ever-more glorious picture of the joys of suburban living, and the prosperity which persisted during those years made it economically feasible for many women to spend their time in what, for some at any rate, seemed like domestic triviality. By the late fifties rumblings of discontent began to be heard, and then in 1963 a suburban housewife published a book the title of which has become part of the language. The heat of the discussions this book aroused suggested the depth of feeling it provoked in both men and women. The introductory paragraphs are printed here.

The problem lay buried, unspoken, for many years in the minds of American women. It was a strange stirring, a sense of dissatisfaction, a yearning that women suffered in the middle of the twentieth century in the United States. Each suburban wife struggled with it alone. As she made the beds, shopped for groceries, matched slip-cover material, ate peanut butter sandwiches with her children,

Betty Friedan, The Feminine Mystique (New York: W. W. Norton & Co., Inc., 1963), pp. 15–19. Copyright © 1963 by Betty Friedan. Reprinted by permission of the publisher.

chauffeured Cub Scouts and Brownies, lay beside her husband at night—she was afraid to ask even of herself the silent question—"Is this all?"

For over fifteen years there was no word of this yearning in the millions of words written about women, for women, in all the columns, books and articles by experts telling women their role was to seek fulfillment as wives and mothers. Over and over women heard in voices of tradition and of Freudian sophistication that they could desire no greater destiny than to glory in their own femininity. Experts told them how to catch a man and keep him, how to breastfeed children and handle their toilet training, how to cope with sibling rivalry and adolescent rebellion; how to buy a dishwasher, bake bread, cook gourmet snails, and build a swimming pool with their own hands; how to dress, look, and act more feminine and make marriage more exciting; how to keep their husbands from dying young and their sons from growing into delinquents. They were taught to pity the neurotic, unfeminine, unhappy women who wanted to be poets or physicists or presidents. They learned that truly feminine women do not want careers, higher education, political rights—the independence and the opportunities that the old-fashioned feminists fought for. Some women, in their forties and fifties, still remembered painfully giving up those dreams, but most of the younger women no longer even thought about them. A thousand expert voices applauded their femininity, their adjustment, their new maturity. All they had to do was devote their lives from earliest girlhood to finding a husband and bearing children.

By the end of the nineteen-fifties, the average marriage age of women in America dropped to 20, and was still dropping, into the teens. Fourteen million girls were engaged by 17. The proportion of women attending college in comparison with men dropped from 47 percent in 1920 to 35 percent in 1950. A century earlier, women had fought for higher education; now girls went to college to get a husband. By the mid-fifties, 60 percent dropped out of college to marry, or because they were afraid too much education would be a marriage bar. Colleges built dormitories for "married students," but the students were almost always the husbands. A new degree was instituted for the wives—"Ph.T." (Putting Husband Through).

Then American girls began getting married in high school. And the women's magazines, deploring the unhappy statistics about these young marriages, urged that courses on marriage, and marriage counselors, be installed in the high schools. Girls started going steady at twelve and thirteen, in junior high. Manufacturers put out brassieres with false bosoms of foam rubber for little girls of ten. And an advertisement for a child's dress, sizes 3–6x, in the *New York Times* in the fall of 1960, said: "She Too Can Join the Man-Trap Set."

By the end of the fifties, the United States birthrate was overtaking India's. The birth-control movement, renamed Planned Parenthood, was asked to find a method whereby women who had been advised that a third or fourth baby would be born dead or defective might have it anyhow. Statisticians were especially astounded at the fantastic increase in the number of babies among college women. Where once they had two children, now they had four, five, six. Women who had once wanted careers were now making careers out of having babies. So rejoiced *Life* magazine in a 1956 paean to the movement of American women back to the home.

In a New York hospital, a woman had a nervous breakdown when she found she could not breastfeed her baby. In other hospitals, women dying of cancer refused a drug which research had proved might save their lives: its side effects were said to be unfeminine. "If I have only one life, let me live it as a blonde," a larger-than-life-sized picture of a pretty, vacuous woman proclaimed from newspaper, magazine, and drugstore ads. And across America, three out of every ten women dyed their hair blonde. They ate a chalk called Metrecal, instead of food, to shrink to the size of the thin young models. Department-store buyers reported that American women, since 1939, had become three and four sizes smaller. "Women are out to fit the clothes, instead of vice-versa," one buyer said.

Interior decorators were designing kitchens with mosaic murals and original paintings, for kitchens were once again the center of women's lives. Home sewing became a million-dollar industry. Many women no longer left their homes, except to shop, chauffeur their children, or attend a social engagement with their husbands. Girls were growing up in America without ever having jobs outside the home. In the late fifties, a sociological phenomenon was suddenly remarked: a third of American women now worked, but most were no longer young and very few were pursuing careers. They were married women who held part-time jobs, selling or secretarial, to put their husbands through school, their sons through college, or to help pay the mortgage. Or they were widows supporting families. Fewer and fewer women were entering professional work. The shortages in the nursing, social work, and teaching professions caused crises in almost every American city. Concerned over the Soviet Union's lead in the space race, scientists noted that America's greatest source of unused brain-power was women. But girls would not study physics: it was "unfeminine." A girl refused a science fellowship at Johns Hopkins to take a job in a real-estate office. All she wanted, she said, was what every other American girl wanted—to get married, have four children and live in a nice house in a nice suburb.

The suburban housewife—she was the dream image of the young American women and the envy, it was said, of women all over the world. The American housewife—freed by science and labor-saving appliances from the drudgery, the dangers of childbirth and the illnesses of her grandmother. She was healthy, beautiful, educated, concerned only about her husband, her children, her home. She had found true feminine fulfillment. As a housewife and mother, she was respected as a full and equal partner to man in his world. She was free to choose automobiles, clothes, appliances, supermarkets; she had everything that women ever dreamed of.

In the fifteen years after World War II, this mystique of feminine fulfillment became the cherished and self-perpetuating core of contemporary American culture. Millions of women lived their lives in the image of those pretty pictures of the American suburban housewife, kissing their husbands goodbye in front of the picture window, depositing their stationwagonsful of children at school, and smiling as they ran the new electric waxer over the spotless kitchen floor. They baked their own bread, sewed their own and their children's clothes, kept their new washing machines and dryers running all day. They changed the sheets on the beds twice a week instead of once, took the rug-hooking class in adult education, and pitied their poor frustrated mothers, who had dreamed of having a career. Their only dream was to be perfect wives and mothers; their highest ambition to have five children and a beautiful house, their only fight to get and keep their husbands. They had no thought for the unfeminine problems of the world outside the home; they wanted the men to make the major decisions. They gloried in their role as women, and wrote proudly on the census blank: "Occupation: housewife."

For over fifteen years, the words written for women, and the words women used when they talked to each other, while their husbands sat on the other side of the room and talked shop or politics or septic tanks, were about problems with their children, or how to keep their husbands happy, or improve their children's school, or cook chicken or make slipcovers. Nobody argued whether women were inferior or superior to men; they were simply different. Words like "emancipation" and "career" sounded strange and embarrassing; no one had used them for years. When a Frenchwoman named Simone de Beauvoir wrote a book called *The Second Sex*, an American critic commented that she obviously "didn't know what life was all about," and besides, she was talking about French women. The "woman problem" in America no longer existed.

If a woman had a problem in the 1950's and 1960's, she knew that something must be wrong with her marriage, or with herself. Other women were satisfied with their lives, she thought. What kind of a woman was she if she did not feel this mysterious fulfillment waxing the kitchen floor? She was so ashamed to admit her dissatisfaction that she never knew how many other women shared it. If she tried to tell her husband, he didn't understand what she was talking about. She did not really understand it herself. For over fifteen years women in America found it harder to talk about this problem than about sex. Even the psychoanalysts had no name for it. When a woman went to a psychiatrist for help, as many women did, she would say, "I'm so ashamed," or "I must be hopelessly neurotic." "I don't know what's wrong with women today," a suburban psychiatrist said uneasily. "I only know something is wrong because most of my patients happen to be women. And their problem isn't sexual." Most women with this problem did not go to see a psychoanalyst, however. "There's nothing wrong really," they kept telling themselves. "There isn't any problem."

But on an April morning in 1959, I heard a mother of four, having coffee with four other mothers in a suburban development fifteen miles from New York, say in a tone of quiet desperation, "the problem." And the others knew, without words, that she was not talking about a problem with her husband, or her children, or her home. Suddenly they realized they all shared the same problem, the problem that has no name. They began, hesitantly, to talk about it. Later, after they had picked up their children at nursery school and taken them home to nap, two of the women cried, in sheer relief, just to know they were not alone.

CREATIVE WOMEN AND MEN AND MARRIAGE

*A year after Mrs. Friedan's book appeared, Marya Mannes,
a free-lance writer and lecturer, told a symposium in California
that creative women suffered also from the pressures to be
truly feminine.*

. . . But most of us who produce in the realm of thought and
ideas cannot do and be all these things and should not try. Evidence
abounds that even the supposedly contented suburban housewife
with four children and no aspirations beyond her home is a victim
of this multiplicity of roles. In the process of trying to be mother,
wife, lover, chef, servant, and hostess, she apparently consumes
alarming quantities of tranquilizers and alcohol—surely not an index of fulfillment. Yet those of us who aspire creatively struggle as
she does to prove to the world that we too are feminine and, therefore, desirable.

This, I maintain, is a sort of craven appeasement that does no
honor to a free intelligence. For the fact is, we cannot have our cake
and eat it, too. We cannot enjoy our mobility, our resources, our
liberties, our triumphs, our intense and heady involvements without
paying for them. And these are some of the prices: The first is popu-
larity. At school the brilliant, intense girl student with dreams in her
head isn't going to get the boys unless her attractions are strong
enough to deceive them. In this case she will probably get the wrong
boys, for the right ones won't be ready for her. This is probably the
right place to say that beauty is possibly the greatest hazard of a
creative woman to herself as well as to its victims. Male adoration is
a powerful deterrent to female sense, and it is extremely difficult to
tear oneself from loving arms and say, "Sorry, darling, I've got to
work." It is so much easier and pleasanter to drown in current
delights than gird for future dreams. Also, beauty demands a degree
of maintenance, and it is the strong woman who turns her back
on the hairdresser to gain two extra hours of work. Certainly, creative labor has been a compensation in many women of talent for the

*Marya Mannes, "The Problems of Creative Women," in Wilson and Farber,
eds.,* The Potential of Woman *(New York: McGraw-Hill, 1963), pp. 124–25.
Copyright © 1963 by McGraw-Hill, Inc. Reprinted by permission of the publisher.*

attractions they lack, and there is no doubt that homeliness permits a dedication and continuity which beauty fragments. In this case, the advance of middle age can be a boon: as the lines increase, the distractions dwindle, and seduction can be more easily confined to the typewriter or microscope.

After school or college, the creative young woman seriously concerned with work will have to realize that marriage with the wrong man can be worse than no marriage. While all her sisters are marching down the aisle at nineteen and twenty for the sake of being married, she must have the nerve to resist the stampede and give herself time to learn, to experience, to grow in the direction of her free dreams. Above all, she must not be afraid of singleness or even loneliness, for I know of no woman, let alone man, who has any stature or worth without knowledge of either. It is the insecure and the immature who cannot bear the thought of their own singularity, who must hold on to another hand from puberty onward, who surround themselves with human buffers against the world.

Since vitality and curiosity are essential equipments of a creative woman, she must be willing to pay the price of trial and error—loving men who may not love her, being loved by men she cannot love. If she is worried about what others think of her, by what standards of morality she is judged, she will not stand the gaff of independence long.

If she marries, soon or late, she will be wise to find the man with sufficient female sensitivity to match her masculine liberty—for the kind of man who has to prove his masculinity through domination is not for her. She will therefore be inordinately lucky if she finds one of the relatively few men whose security lies in the full and equal partnership of a love which may—or may not—produce children.

If she has children—this creative woman of ours—she must pay for this indulgence with a long burden of guilt, for her life will be split three ways between them and her husband and her work. What she gives to one she must take from the other, and there will be no time when one or the other is not harmed. No woman with any heart can compose a paragraph when her child is in trouble or her husband ill: forever they take precedence over the companions of her mind. In this, as in many other things, the creative woman has a much tougher time than the creative man. For one thing, she has no wife, as he has, to protect her from intrusion, to maintain the machinery of living, to care for the children, to answer the doorbell. For another, no one believes her time to be sacred. A man at his desk in a room with a closed door is a man at work. A woman at a desk in any room is available.

A NEW RADICALISM

The resurgence of feminism signaled by Mrs. Friedan's book and a number of other developments, such as the appointment by President Kennedy of a Commission on the Status of Women, and the proliferation of programs for continuing education, continued through the sixties. By the end of the decade there were signs of a new radicalism, especially among young women. The ancient discontent over job and wage discrimination linked to a protest against the psychology of inferiority sparked a large number of spontaneous groups collectively described as the Woman's Liberation Movement. Some of these groups were austerely concerned with legal rights. Others were more flamboyant, expressing dramatically women's discontent with a male-dominated society. Among the proliferating manifestoes this one by the Redstockings, a self-styled group of radical feminists, gives some idea of the new elements in contemporary feminism.

1. After centuries of individual and preliminary political struggle, women are uniting to achieve their final liberation from male supremacy. Redstockings is dedicated to building this unity and winning our freedom.

2. Women are an oppressed class. Our oppression is total, affecting every facet of our lives. We are exploited as sex objects, breeders, domestic servants, and cheap labor. We are considered inferior beings, whose only purpose is to enhance men's lives. Our humanity is denied. Our prescribed behavior is enforced by the threat of physical violence.

Because we have lived so intimately with our oppressors, in isolation from each other, we have been kept from seeing our personal suffering as a political condition. This creates the illusion that a woman's relationship with her man is a matter of interplay between

"Redstockings Manifesto," printed in Notes From the Second Year, Women's Liberation: Major Writings of the Radical Feminists.

two unique personalities, and can be worked out individually. In reality, every such relationship is a *class* relationship, and the conflicts between individual men and women are *political* conflicts that can only be solved collectively.

3. We identify the agents of our oppression as men. Male supremacy is the oldest, most basic form of domination. All other forms of exploitation and oppression (racism, capitalism, imperialism, etc.) are extensions of male supremacy: men dominate women, a few men dominate the rest. All power structures throughout history have been male-dominated and male-oriented. Men have controlled all political, economic and cultural institutions and backed up this control with physical force. They have used their power to keep women in an inferior position. *All men* receive economic, sexual, and psychological benefits from male supremacy. *All men* have oppressed women.

4. Attempts have been made to shift the burden of responsibility from men to institutions or to women themselves. We condemn these arguments as evasions. Institutions alone do not oppress; they are merely tools of the oppressor. To blame institutions implies that men and women are equally victimized, obscures the fact that men benefit from the subordination of women, and gives men the excuse that they are forced to be oppressors. On the contrary, any man is free to renounce his superior position provided that he is willing to be treated like a woman by other men.

We also reject the idea that women consent to or are to blame for their own oppression. Women's submission is not the result of brainwashing, stupidity, or mental illness but of continual, daily pressure from men. We do not need to change ourselves, but to change men.

The most slanderous evasion of all is that women can oppress men. The basis for this illusion is the isolation of individual relationships from their political context and the tendency of men to see any legitimate challenge to their privileges as persecution.

5. We regard our personal experience, and our feelings about that experience, as the basis for an analysis of our common situation. We cannot rely on existing ideologies as they are all products of male supremacist culture. We question every generalization and accept none that are not confirmed by our experience.

Our chief task at present is to develop female class consciousness through sharing experience and publicly exposing the sexist foundation of all our institutions. Consciousness-raising is not "therapy," which implies the existence of individual solutions and falsely assumes that the male-female relationship is purely personal, but the only method by which we can ensure that our program for liberation is based on the concrete realities of our lives.

The first requirement for raising class consciousness is honesty, in private and in public, with ourselves and other women.

6. We identify with all women. We define our best interest as that of the poorest, most brutally exploited woman.

We repudiate all economic, racial, educational or status privileges that divide us from other women. We are determined to recognize and eliminate any prejudices we may hold against other women.

We are committed to achieving internal democracy. We will do whatever is necessary to ensure that every woman in our movement has an equal chance to participate, assume responsibility, and develop her political potential.

7. We call on all our sisters to unite with us in struggle.

We call on all men to give up their male privileges and support women's liberation in the interest of our humanity and their own.

In fighting for our liberation we will always take the side of women against their oppressors. We will not ask what is "revolutionary" or "reformist," only what is good for women.

The time for individual skirmishes has passed. This time we are going all the way.

July 7, 1969

ANDROGYNY?

Many new directions for women have emerged from the changes of the past century, and nobody has a very good crystal ball in which to see what the future holds. Caroline Bird, in a recent book, takes a look in hers.

. . . People can be classified in all sorts of ways. The easiest and the oldest way is to divide the human race into male and female.

Caroline Bird, Born Female: The High Cost of Keeping Women Down *(New York: David McKay Company, Inc., 1968), pp. ix–xii. Copyright © 1968 by Caroline Bird. Reprinted by permission of the publisher.*

But people can also be classified according to the way *they* classify people.

Some views of life are founded on the difference between the sexes. The worlds of Sigmund Freud, Sir Lancelot, Tarzan, Richard Rodgers, Scheherazade, and the Lone Ranger elaborate the celebrated difference.

Other symbolic figures aren't "sexist" in this way. Benjamin Franklin, the Beatles, Eleanor Roosevelt, Shakespeare, Svetlana Alliluyeva are not sexless individuals, but they have made a great many statements about people which apply to men as well as to women. In their worlds, people have been and are classified on the basis of insight, politics, skills, and interests, and their pigeonholes are coeducational. Their ideal person combines characteristics usually attributed to men with characteristics usually attributed to women; he is, as the Greek word goes, "androgynous."

After a long period of celebrating the differences between men and women, we are heading into an androgynous world in which the most important thing about a person will no longer be his or her sex. The notion sounds unbearably dull and even blasphemous to everyone over thirty, the age at which, according to the new young, adults become untrustworthy. But how many culture heroes of the young now parade or exploit their masculinity or femininity? Teenagers have abandoned Richard Rodgers for the socially-conscious songs of Joan Baez, and Sophia Loren does not excite the young admirers of Twiggy.

Twiggy closely resembles her "companion," not husband, beau or boyfriend. Both wear their hair much the same way—except that his is longer. Both take an equal interest in decorating their persons. And they are companions because they are usually doing the same thing—riding a motorcycle or rocking to the beat of music which provides a climate for a mob rather than the key to a private world for two. The hippies and the psychedelic experimenters call the old-fashioned kind of sexual love egotistical. They want to break out of the small-family grouping. In the Haight-Ashbury section of San Francisco and in the East Village of New York their open communes are dedicated to a more generalized kind of love than is celebrated by Rodgers and Hammerstein.

Androgyny is not confined to the hippies. In the jungles of Asia and Africa, in our own primitive Kentucky mountains, boys and girls go out to help the disadvantaged, wearing identical clothes, living in tents or huts, or with the people they have come to aid. Newlyweds from privileged families often choose this conspicuously unprivate trip as a honeymoon. The style is everything young intellectuals admire: humanitarian, austere, dangerous, uncomfortable—and androgynous. Arm-in-arm, they seem to be saying that they enjoy the similarity of their experience as much as the possibilities for pleasure in their anatomical difference.

In 1967, a Radcliffe girl and a Harvard boy took an apartment together and allowed a magazine to print their pictures and their names. The rebellion against marriage is familiar, but past rebels have lived together as man and wife. The youngsters pictured are living together as roommates. "He cooks," the caption on their picture read. "She irons. They do the laundry together."

These responsible young students are not revolting against the responsibilities of marriage so much as against the premise of the institution. What the long-haired boys and the shiny-nosed girls seem to be telegraphing is a declaration of independence from sex roles. "We don't think men should be shackled to desks and machines in order to prove that they are men," they seem to be saying. "We don't think girls should have to limit their interests in order to prove that they are women. As a matter of fact, we happen to think that traditional marriage is as corrupt as prostitution. It's based on economics, not love."

The contraceptive pill may reduce the importance of sex not only as a basis for the division of labor, but as a guideline in developing talents and interests. "It is most doubtful, in the new age, that the rigidly 'male' qualities will be of much use," Marshall McLuhan wrote in 1967. "In fact, there may well be little need for standardized males or females. . . . The whole business of sex may become again, as in the tribal state, play—freer, but less important."

Margaret Mead, the most reliable bellwether for changes in man-woman relationships over the past thirty years, now suggests that the family of the future won't even be based on sex or a sexual relationship. Many people will get the emotional reassurance now provided by marriage from individuals of the same or opposite sex who are *simpatico* rather than sexually compelling. Housemates may or may not be sex mates. This is the far-out thinking of 1968.

David Riesman, the Harvard sociologist, puts the new ideal in sociological language. "I think what I would ideally like to see in our society is that sex become an ascribed rather than an achieved status," he told an audience of college girls. "That one is simply born a girl or a boy and that's it. And no worry about an activity's defeminizing or emasculating one." In this brave new world, babies would not be committed to a specific adult role because they happened to be *born female*. Sex would be a personal characteristic of only slightly more consequence than the color of one's hair, eyes—or skin.

Sex is here to stay, but its future is in private life, not in the office. Sex is becoming a less useful way to classify workers and organize work, yet the sex lines are still maintained in offices and plants and women are still penalized on the job by unexamined assumptions about their family roles.

This [*Born Female*] is a frankly feminist book. It counts the social, moral, and personal costs of keeping women down on the job and finds them high:

We are destroying talent. The price of occupational success is made so high for women that barring exceptional luck only the unusually talented or frankly neurotic can afford to succeed. Girls size up the bargain early and turn it down.

We are wasting talent. The able workers that employers say they can't find are all too often in their own back rooms or lofts doing jobs that use only a fraction of their ability.

We are hiding talent. Some of our brightest citizens are quietly tucked away at home, their aptitudes concealed by the label "Housewife."

The young see these costs, and some are refusing to pay them. Men and women of the future will share the work of home and shop on the basis of individual abilities and convenience. The discriminations *for and against* women in general are fading, but they are not fading fast enough to keep up with the changing conditions of home and work.

Change always hurts, but change in sex roles hurts women more than men. This book contends that women should not have to suffer all the pain and do all of the adjusting.

We are all in this life together.